EYEWITNESS TRAVEL
GERMAN
VISUAL
PHRASE BOOK

A Dorling Kindersley Book

LONDON, NEW YORK, MELBOURNE,
MUNICH, DELHI

Senior Editor Angela Wilkes
Art Editor Silke Spingies
Production Editor Lucy Baker
Production Controller Inderjit Bhullar
Managing Editor Julie Oughton
Managing Art Editor Christine Keilty
Reference Publisher Jonathan Metcalf
Art Director Bryn Walls

Produced for Dorling Kindersley by
SP Creative Design
Editor Heather Thomas
Designer Rolando Ugolino

Language content for Dorling Kindersley
by First Edition Translations Ltd,
Cambridge, UK
Translator Ingrid Price-Gschlossl
Editor Tamara Benscheidt
Typesetting Essential Typesetting

First published in Great Britain in 2008
by Dorling Kindersley Limited,
80 Strand, London WC2R 0RL

A Penguin Company

4 6 8 10 9 7 5 3
004 - ED639 - July/09
Copyright © Dorling Kindersley Ltd 2008

A CIP catalogue record for this book is
available from the British Library

ISBN: 978-1-4053-3226-2

Printed by Leo Paper China

Discover more at
www.dk.com

CONTENTS

INTRODUCTION

This book provides all the key words and phrases you are
likely to need in everyday situations. It is grouped into
themes, and key phrases are broken down into short
sections, to help you build a wide variety of sentences.
A lot of the vocabulary is illustrated to make it easy to
remember, and "You may hear" boxes feature questions
you are likely to hear. At the back of the book there is a
menu guide, listing about 500 food terms, and a 2,000-
word two-way dictionary. Numbers and the most useful
phrases are listed on the jacket flaps for quick reference.

Nouns

All German nouns (words for things, people, and ideas)
are masculine, feminine, or neuter. The gender of singular
nouns is shown by the word for "the": **der** (masculine),
die (feminine), or **das** (neuter). **Die** is also used with
plural nouns. You can look up the gender of words in the
German–English dictionary at the back of the book. Some
nouns, such as people's jobs or nationalities, change
endings according to whether you are talking about a man
or woman. In this book the masculine form is usually
shown, followed by the feminine form:

I'm English   **Ich bin Engländer/Engländerin**

"A"

The word for "a" or "an" also changes according to gender.
It is **ein** for masculine and neuter words and **eine** for
feminine words. Alternatives are shown as below:

Another…please   **Noch ein/eine…bitte**

"You"

There are two ways of saying "you" when addressing
someone in German: **Sie** (polite) and **du** (familiar). In this
book we have used **Sie** throughout as this is what you
normally use with people you don't know.

Pronunciation guide

Below each German word or phrase in this book, you will find a pronunciation guide. Read it as if it were English and you should be understood, but remember that it is only a guide and for the best results you should listen to and mimic native speakers. Some German sounds are different from those in English, so take note of how the letters below are pronounced.

a	like a in father
ä	like e in get
au	like ow in how
äu, eu	like oy in toy
b	like b at the beginning of a word
	like p at the end of a word
ch	pronounced at the back of the throat, like ch in the Scottish word loch
d	like d in dog at the beginning of a word
	like t in tin at the end of a word
ei	like y in by, or i in pile
i	like i in hit, or ee in see
ie	like ee in see
j	like y in yes
ö	like ur in burn
qu	like kv
r	rolled at the back of the throat
s	like s in see, sh in ship, or z in zoo
sch	like sh in shop
ß	like ss in grass
u	like oo in boot
ü	like ew in dew
v	like f in foot
w	like v in van
z	like ts in pets

ESSENTIALS

In this section, you will find the essential words and phrases you will need for basic everyday talk and situations. Be aware of cultural differences when you are addressing native German speakers, and remember that they tend to be quite formal when greeting each other. There are two ways of saying "you" in German. *Sie* is used for older people or ones you don't know very well, whereas the more familiar *du* is used with family and friends.

GREETINGS

Hello	Guten Tag! *goo-ten tahk*
Good evening	Guten Abend *goo-ten ah-bent*
Good night	Gute Nacht *goo-te nakht*
Goodbye	Auf Wiedersehen *owf vee-der-zay-en*
Hi/bye!	Tschüss! *tshews*
Pleased to meet you	Sehr erfreut *zair air-froyt*
How are you?	Wie geht es Ihnen? *vee gayt es ee-nen*
Fine, thanks	Danke, gut *dun-ke goot*
You're welcome	Nichts zu danken *nikhts tsoo dun-ken*
My name is...	Ich heiße... *ikh hye-se*
What's your name?	Wie heißen Sie? *vee hye-sen zee*
What's his/her name?	Wie heißt er/sie? *vee hyst air/zee*
This is...	Das ist... *dus ist*
Nice to meet you	Freut mich *froyt mikh*
See you tomorrow	Bis morgen *bis mor-gen*
See you soon	Bis bald *bis bahlt*

SMALL TALK

Yes/no	Ja/Nein *yah/nine*
Please	Bitte *bit-te*
Thank you (very much)	Danke (vielen Dank) *dun-ke (vee-len dunk)*
You're welcome	Gern geschehen *gairn ge-shay-en*
OK/fine	OK/prima *o-kay/pree-ma*
Pardon?	Wie bitte? *vee bit-te*
Excuse me	Entschuldigung *ent-shool-dee-gung*
Sorry	Tut mir leid *toot mir lite*
I don't know	Ich weiß es nicht *ikh vice es nikht*
I don't understand	Ich verstehe Sie nicht *ikh fair-shtay-ye zee nikht*
Could you repeat that?	Könnten Sie das wiederholen? *kurn-ten zee dus vee-der-ho-len*
I don't speak German	Ich spreche nicht Deutsch *ikh shpray-khe nikht doytsh*
Do you speak English?	Sprechen Sie Englisch? *shpray-ken zee eng-lish*
What is the German for...?	Was heißt...auf Deutsch? *vus hyst...owf doytsh*
What's that?	Was ist das? *vus ist dus*
What's that called?	Wie heißt das? *vee hyst dus*
Can you tell me...	Können Sie mir sagen... *kurnen zee mir zah-gen*

TALKING ABOUT YOURSELF

I'm from…	Ich komme aus… *ikh kom-me ows*
I'm…	Ich bin… *ikh bin*
…English	…Engländer/Engländerin *eng-len-der/eng-len-der-in*
…American	…Amerikaner/Amerikanerin *ah-meri-kah-ner/ ah-meri-kah-ner-in*
…Canadian	…Kanadier/Kanadierin *kah-nah-dee-er/ kah-nah-dee-er-in*
…Australian	…Australier/Australierin *ows-trah-lee-er/ ows-trah-lee-er-in*
…single/married	…ledig/verheiratet *leh-dik/fair-hy-ra-tet*
…divorced	…geschieden *ge-shee-den*
I am…years old	Ich bin…Jahre alt *ikh bin…yah-re ult*
I have…	Ich habe… *ikh hah-be*
…a boyfriend	…einen Freund *ine-en froynt*
…a girlfriend	…eine Freundin *ine-e froyn-din*

You may hear…

- **Wo kommen Sie her?**
  vo kom-men zee hair
  Where are you from?

- **Sind Sie verheiratet?**
  zint zee fair-hy-ra-tet
  Are you married?

- **Haben Sie Kinder?**
  hah-ben zee kin-der
  Do you have children?

SOCIALIZING

Do you live here?	Wohnen Sie hier? *voh-nen zee heer*
Where do you live?	Wo wohnen Sie? *vo voh-nen zee*
I am here...	Ich bin hier... *ikh bin heer*
...on holiday	...im Urlaub *im oor-lowp*
...on business	...auf Dienstreise *owf deenst-rye-ze*
I'm a student	Ich bin Student/Studentin *ikh bin shtoo-dent/ shtoo-den-tin*
I work in...	Ich arbeite in/im... *ikh ar-by-te in/im*
I am retired	Ich bin in Pension *ikh bin in pen-zee-on*
Can I...	Kann ich... *kunn ikh*
...have your telephone number?	...Ihre Telefonnummer haben? *ee-re tay-lay-fohn-noom-mer hah-ben*
...have your email address?	...Ihre E-Mailadrese haben? *ee-re e-mail-ah-dres-se hah-ben*
It doesn't matter	Das macht nichts *dus makht nikhts*
Cheers	Prost *prost*
I don't drink/smoke	Ich trinke/rauche nicht *ikh trin-ke/row-khe nikht*
Are you alright?	Wie geht es Ihnen? *vee gayt es ee-nen*
I'm OK	Es geht mir gut *es gayt mir goot*
What do you think?	Was denken Sie? *vus den-ken zee*

LIKES AND DISLIKES

I like/love...	Ich mag/liebe... *ikh mahk/lee-be*
I don't like...	Ich mag keinen/keine/kein... *ikh mahk kine-en/kine-e/ kine*
I hate...	Ich hasse... *ikh has-se*
I quite/really like...	Ich habe...ganz/sehr gern *ikh hah-be...gunts/zair gern*
Don't you like it?	Mögen Sie das nicht? *mur-gen zee dus nikht*
I would like...	Ich möchte gern... *ikh murkh-te gairn*
I'd like this one/that one	Ich möchte das hier/dort *ikh murkh-te dus heer/dort*
My favourite is...	Am liebsten mag ich... *um leep-sten mahk ikh*
I prefer...	Ich mag lieber... *ikh mahk lee-ber*
I think it's great/awful	Ich finde es toll/schrecklich *ikh fin-de es toll/shrek-likh*
What would you like to do?	Was möchten Sie gern tun? *vus murkh-ten zee gairn toon*

You may hear...

- **Was machen Sie?**
  vus makhen zee
  What do you do?

- **Sind Sie im Urlaub?**
  zint zee im oor-lowp
  Are you on holiday?

- **Mögen Sie...?**
  mur-gen zee
  Do you like...?

DAYS OF THE WEEK

What day is it today?	Welcher Tag ist heute? *vel-kher tahk ist hoy-te*
Sunday	Sonntag *zon-tahk*
Monday	Montag *mohn-tahk*
Tuesday	Dienstag *deens-tahk*
Wednesday	Mittwoch *mit-vokh*
Thursday	Donnerstag *don-ners-tahk*
Friday	Freitag *fry-tahk*
Saturday	Samstag *zums-tahk*
today	heute *hoy-te*
tomorrow	morgen *mor-gen*
yesterday	gestern *ges-tairn*
in…days	in…Tagen *in…tah-gen*

THE SEASONS

der Frühling
dair frew-ling
spring

der Sommer
dair zom-mer
summer

MONTHS

January	Januar *yunn-oo-ahr*
February	Februar *fay-broo-ahr*
March	März *mairts*
April	April *ah-pril*
May	Mai *my*
June	Juni *yoo-nee*
July	Juli *yoo-lee*
August	August *ow-goost*
September	September *zep-tem-bair*
October	Oktober *ok-toe-bair*
November	November *no-vem-bair*
December	Dezember *day-tsem-bair*

der Herbst
dair hairpst
autumn

der Winter
dair vin-ter
winter

TELLING THE TIME

What time is it?	Wie spät ist es? *vee shpayt ist es*
It's nine o'clock	Es ist neun Uhr *es ist noyn oor*
...in the morning	...morgens *mor-gens*
...in the afternoon	...am Nachmittag *um nakh-mit-tahk*
...in the evening	...abends *ah-bents*

ein Uhr
ine oor
one o'clock

zehn nach eins
tsayn nakh ines
ten past one

Viertel nach eins
feer-tel nakh ines
quarter past one

zwanzig nach eins
tsvun-tsik nakh ines
twenty past one

halb zwei
hulp tsvy
half past one

Viertel vor zwei
feer-tel for tsvy
quarter to two

zehn Minuten vor zwei
tsayn mee-noo-ten for tsvy
ten to two

zwei Uhr
tsvy oor
two o'clock

It's midday/midnight	Es ist Mittag/Mitternacht *es ist mit-tahk/mit-ter-nakht*
second	die Sekunde *dee ze-koon-de*
minute	die Minute *dee mee-noo-te*
hour	die Stunde *dee shtoon-de*
a quarter of an hour	eine Viertelstunde *ine-e feer-tel-shtoon-de*
half an hour	die halbe Stunde *dee hul-be shtoon-de*
three-quarters of an hour	die Dreiviertelstunde *dee dry-feer-tel-shtoon-de*
late	spät *shpayt*
early/soon	früh/bald *frew/bahlt*
What time does it start?	Wann beginnt es? *vun be-ginnt es*
What time does it finish?	Wann endet es? *vun en-det es*
How long will it last?	Wie lange wird es dauern? *vee lun-ghe veert es dow-ern*

You may hear...

- **Bis später.**
  bis shpay-ter
  See you later.

- **Sie sind früh dran.**
  zee zint frew drun
  You're early.

- **Sie sind spät dran.**
  zee zint shpayt drun
  You're late.

THE WEATHER

What's the forecast?	Wie ist der Wetterbericht? *vee ist dair vet-ter-be-rikht*
What's the weather like?	Wie ist das Wetter? *vee ist dus vet-ter*
It's...	Es ist... *es ist*
...good	...schön *shurn*
...bad	...schlecht *shlekht*
...warm	...warm *varm*
...hot	...heiß *hys*
...cold	...kalt *kult*
...humid	...schwül *shvewl*

Es ist sonnig
es ist zon-nik
It's sunny

Es regnet
es reg-net
It's raining

Es ist wolkig
es ist vol-kik
It's cloudy

Es ist stürmisch
es ist shtewr-mish
It's stormy

What's the temperature?	Wie viele Grad hat es? *vee fee-le graht hut es*
It's...degrees	Es hat...Grad *es hut...graht*
It's a beautiful day	Es ist ein schöner Tag *es ist ine shur-ner tahk*
The weather's changing	Es ist veränderlich *es ist fair-en-der-likh*
Is it going to get colder/ hotter?	Wird es kälter/wärmer? *veert es kel-ter/vehr-mer*
It's cooling down	Es kühlt ab *es kewlt up*
Is it going to freeze?	Wird es eisig? *veert es eye-zik*

Es schneit
es shnyt
It's snowing

Es ist eisig
es ist eye-zik
It's icy

Es ist neblig
es ist neb-lik
It's misty

Es ist windig
es ist vin-dik
It's windy

GETTING AROUND

Germany has an excellent road and motorway (*Autobahn*) system if you are travelling around the country by car. German trains are fast and punctual, linking the main urban centres. In larger towns and cities, you can usually get around by taxi or through the integrated transport system of trams, buses and, sometimes, underground railways (*U-Bahn*). All you need to do is to buy a ticket in advance and then validate it when you travel.

ASKING WHERE THINGS ARE

Excuse me, please	Entschuldigen Sie, bitte *ent-shool-di-gen zee bit-te*
Where is...	Wo ist... *vo ist*
...the town centre?	...das Stadtzentrum? *dus shtut-tsen-troom*
...the railway station?	...der Bahnhof? *dair bahn-hohf*
...a cash machine?	...ein Geldautomat? *ine gelt-ow-toe-mat*
How do I get to...?	Wie komme ich zu...? *vee kom-me ikh tsoo*
I'm going to the railway station	Ich gehe zum Bahnhof *ikh gay-e tsoom bahn-hohf*
I'm looking for a restaurant	Ich suche nach einem Restaurant *ikh zookhe nahkh ine-em res-to-rung*
I'm lost	Ich habe mich verlaufen *ikh hah-be mikh fair-low-fen*
Is it near?	Ist es nicht weit? *ist es nikht vyte*
Is there a bank nearby?	Ist eine Bank in der Nähe? *ist ine-e bunk in dair nay-he*
Is it far?	Ist es weit? *ist es vyte*
How far is...	Wie weit ist es... *vee vyte ist es*
...the town hall?	...zum Rathaus? *tsoom raht-hows*
...the market?	...zum Markt? *tsoom markt*
Can I walk there?	Kann ich zu Fuß hingehen? *kunn ikh tsoo foos hin-gay-en*

CAR RENTAL

Where is the car rental desk?	Wo ist der Mietwagenschalter? *vo ist dair* *meet-vahgen-shal-ter*
I want to hire…	Ich möchte…mieten *ikh murkh-te…mee-ten*
…a car	…ein Auto *ine ow-toe*
…a motorbike	…ein Motorrad *ine mo-tor-raht*
…a bicycle	…ein Fahrrad *ine far-raht*

die Limousine
dee lee-mo-zee-ne
saloon car

das Hecktürmodell
dus heck-tewr-mo-dell
hatchback

das Motorrad
dus mo-tor-raht
motorbike

der Motorroller
dair mo-tor-roll-ler
scooter

das Mountainbike
dus mountain-bike
mountain bike

das Rennrad
dus ren-raht
road bike

…for…days	…für…Tage *fewr…tah-ge*
…for a week	…für eine Woche *fewr ine-e vo-khe*

...for the weekend	...für das Wochenende *fewr dus vo-khen-end-e*
I'd like...	Ich möchte... *ikh murkh-te*
...an automatic	...einen Wagen mit Automatikgetriebe *ine-en vahgen mit ow-toe-matik-ge-tree-be*
...a manual	...einen Wagen mit Handschaltung *ine-en vahgen mit hunt-shal-tung*
Has it got air conditioning?	Hat er eine Klimaanlage? *hut air ine-e kleema-an- lahge*
Should I return it with a full tank?	Soll ich den Wagen vollgetankt zurückbringen? *zoll ikh dain vahgen foll-ge- tunkt tsoo-rewk-brin-gen*
Here's my driving licence	Hier ist mein Führerschein *heer ist mine few-rer-shine*
Do you have a bicycle?	Haben Sie ein Fahrrad? *hah-ben zee ine far-raht*

der Kindersitz
dair kin-der-zits
child seat

der Fahrradhelm
dair far-raht-helm
cycle helmet

das Fahrradschloss
dus far-raht-shlos
lock

die Fahrradpumpe
dee far-raht-poom-pe
bicycle pump

DRIVING

Is this the road to the station?	Ist das die Straße zum Bahnhof? *ist dus dee shtrah-se tsoom bahn-hohf*
Where is the nearest garage?	Wo ist die nächste Werkstatt? *vo ist dee nekh-ste vairk-stut*
I'd like...	Ich hätte gern... *ikh het-te gairn*
...some petrol	...etwas Benzin *et-vas ben-tseen*
...40 litres of unleaded	...40 Liter Bleifrei *feer-tsik lee-ter bly-fry*
...30 litres of diesel	...30 Liter Diesel *dry-sik lee-ter dee-zel*
Fill it up, please	Volltanken bitte *foll-tun-ken bit-te*
Where do I pay?	Wo kann ich zahlen? *vo kunn ikh tsah-len*
The pump number is...	Die Nummer der Zapfsäule ist... *dee noo-mer dair tsapf-zoyle ist*
Can I pay by credit card?	Kann ich mit Kreditkarte zahlen? *kunn ikh mit kray-deet-kar-te tsah-len*

die Tankstelle
dee tunk-shtel-le
petrol station

Please can you check...	Könnten Sie bitte...prüfen *kurn-ten zee bit-te... prew-fen*
...the oil	...das Öl *dus url*
...the tyre pressure	...den Reifendruck *den rye-fen-drook*

PARKING

Is there a car park nearby?	Ist ein Parkplatz in der Nähe? *ist ine park-pluts in dair nay-he*
Can I park here?	Kann ich hier parken? *kunn ikh heer par-ken*
How long can I park for?	Wie lange kann ich parken? *vee lun-ge kunn ikh par-ken*
Is it free?	Ist er gratis? *ist air gra-tis*
How much does it cost?	Wie viel kostet es? *vee feel kos-tet es*
How much is it...	Wie viel kostet es... *vee feel kos-tet es*
...per hour?	...pro Stunde? *pro shtoon-de*
...per day?	...pro Tag? *pro tahk*
...overnight?	...über Nacht? *ew-ber nakht*

der Dachgepäckträger
dair dakh-ge-pek-trayger
roofrack

der Kindersitz
dair kin-der-zits
child seat

THE CAR

der Kofferraum
dair kof-fer-rowm
boot

der Auspuff
dair ows-poof
exhaust

das Rad
dus raht
wheel

die Tür
dee tewr
door

INSIDE THE CAR

die Kopfstütze
dee kopf-shtew-tse
head rest

der Türgriff
dair tewr-griff
handle

das Türschloss
dus tewr-shlos
door lock

der Rücksitz
dair rewk-zits
back seat

der Sicherheitsgurt
dair sikher-hites-goort
seat belt

der Vordersitz
dair vor-dair-zits
front seat

die Windschutzscheibe
dee vint-shoots-shy-be
windscreen

die Motorhaube
dee mo-tor-how-be
bonnet

der Scheinwerfer
dair shyn-vair-fer
headlight

der Reifen
dair rye-fen
tyre

der Motor
dair mo-tor
engine

die Stoßstange
dee shtows-shtange
bumper

THE CONTROLS

der Airbag
dair air-bag
airbag

die Warnblinkleuchte
dee varn-blink-loykhte
hazard lights

das Armaturenbrett
dus arma-tooren-bret
dashboard

das Lenkrad
dus lenk-raht
steering wheel

der Tachometer
dair takho-metair
speedometer

die Benzinuhr
dee ben-tseen-oor
fuel gauge

die Hupe
dee hoo-pe
horn

der Schalthebel
dair shult-hay-bel
gear stick

die Heizung
dee hy-tsoong
heater

das Autoradio
dus ow-toe-rah-deeoh
car stereo

ROAD SIGNS

die Einbahnstraße
dee ine-bahn-shtrah-se
one way

der Kreisverkehr
dair krys-fair-kair
roundabout

Vorfahrt beachten
for-fart be-akh-ten
give way

Parken verboten
par-ken fair-bo-ten
no parking

Einfahrt verboten
ine-fart fair-bo-ten
no entry

Gefahr
ge-far
hazard

Anhalten verboten
un-hul-ten fair-bo-ten
no stopping

Rechtsabbiegen verboten
rekhts-up-bee-gen fair-bo-ten
no right turn

die Geschwindigkeitsbegrenzung
dee ge-shvindik-kyts-be-grentsoong
speed limit

ON THE ROAD

die Parkuhr
dee park-oor
parking meter

die Verkehrsampel
dee fair-kairs-um-pel
traffic light

der Verkehrspolizist
dair fairkairs-polit-sist
traffic policeman

die Straßenkarte
dee shtra-sen-kar-te
map

die Behindertenparkplätze
dee be-hin-der-ten-park-pletse
disabled parking

die Notrufsäule
dee not-roof-zoy-le
emergency phone

der Stau
dair shtow
traffic jam

die Autobahn
dee ow-toe-bahn
motorway

die Zubringerstraße
dee tsoo-brin-ger-shtrah-se
sliproad

AT THE STATION

Where can I buy a ticket?	Wo kann ich eine Fahrkarte kaufen? *voe kunn ikh ine-e far-kar-te kow-fen*
Is there an automatic ticket machine?	Gibt es hier einen Fahrscheinautomaten? *geept es heer ine-en far-shine-owtoe-maten*

der Fahrscheinautomat
dair far-shine-owtoe-mat
automatic ticket machine

die Fahrkarte
dee far-kar-te
ticket

How much is a ticket to…?	Was kostet die Fahrkarte nach…? *vus kos-tet dee far-kar-te nakh*
Two tickets to…	Zwei Fahrkarten nach… *tsvy far-kar-ten nakh*
I'd like…	Ich möchte… *ikh murkh-te*
…a single ticket to…	…eine einfache Fahrkarte nach… *ine-e ine-fakhe far-kar-te nakh*
…a return ticket to…	…eine Rückfahrkarte nach … *ine-e rewk-far-kar-te nakh*
…a first class ticket	…eine Fahrkarte erster Klasse *ine-e far-kar-te air-ster kluss-se*
…a standard class ticket	…eine normale Fahrkarte *ine-e nor-mah-le far-kar-te*

I'd like to…	Ich möchte gern… *ikh murkh-te gairn*
…reserve a seat	…einen Sitzplatz reservieren *ine-en zits-pluts re-zair-vee-ren*
…on the ICE to…	…mit dem ICE nach… *mit daim ee-tseh-ay nakh*
…book a couchette	…einen Liegeplatz reservieren *ine-nen lee-ge-pluts re-zair-vee-ren*
Is there a reduction…?	Gibt es eine Ermäßigung…? *geept es ine-e er-mess-i-goong*
…for children?	…für Kinder? *fewr kin-der*
…for students?	…für Studenten? *fewr shtoo-den-ten*
…for senior citizens?	…für Senioren? *fewr Ze-nee-o-ren*
Is it a fast train?	Ist es ein schneller Zug? *ist es ine shnel-ler tsook*
Do I stamp the ticket before boarding?	Muss ich die Fahrkarte vor dem Einsteigen entwerten? *moos ikh dee far-kar-te for daim ine-shty-gen ent-vair-ten*

You may hear…

- Der Zug fährt von Bahnsteig …ab.
 dair tsook fairt fon bahn-shtyk…up
 The train leaves from platform…

TRAVELLING BY TRAIN

Do you have a timetable?	Haben Sie einen Fahrplan? *hah-ben zee ine-en far-plun*
What time is...	Wann fährt... *vun fairt*
...the next train to...?	...der nächste Zug nach...? *dair nekh-ste tsook nakh*
...the last train to...?	...der letzte Zug nach...? *dair lets-te tsook nakh*
Which platform does it leave from?	Von welchem Bahnsteig fährt er ab? *fon vel-khem bahn-shtyk fairt air up*
What time does it arrive in...?	Wann kommt er in...an? *vun komt air in...un*
How long does it take?	Wie lange dauert die Fahrt? *vee lan-ge dow-ert dee fart*
Is this the train for...?	Ist das dair Zug nach...? *ist das dair tsook nakh*
Is this the right platform for...?	Ist das der richtige Bahnsteig für...? *ist das dair rickh-ti-ge bahn-shtyk fewr*
Where is platform three?	Wo ist Bahnsteig drei? *vo ist bahn-shtyk dry*
Does this train stop at...?	Hält dieser Zug in... ? *helt deezer tsook in*

You may hear...

- **Sie müssen Ihren Fahrschein entwerten.**
  zee mew-sen eer-en far-shine ent-vair-ten
  You must validate your ticket.

- **Benutzen Sie die Maschine.**
  be-noot-sen zee dee ma-shee-ne
  Use the machine.

Where do I change for…?	Wo muss ich nach… umsteigen? *vo moos ikh nakh… oom-shtygen*
Is this seat free?	Ist dieser Platz noch frei? *ist deezer pluts nokh fry*
I've reserved this seat	Ich habe diesen Platz reserviert *ikh hah-be deezen pluts re-zair-veert*
Do I get off here?	Muss ich hier aussteigen? *moos ikh heer ows-shtygen*
Where is the underground station?	Wo ist die U-Bahnstation? *vo ist dee oo-bahn-shta-tsee-on*
Which line goes to…?	Welche Linie fährt nach…? *vel-khe lee-nee-e fairt nakh*

die Bahnhofshalle
dee bahn-hohfs-hull-le
concourse

der Zug
dair tsook
train

der Speisewagen
dair shpy-ze-vahgen
dining car

der Liegeplatz
dair lee-ge-pluts
couchette

BUSES

When is the next bus to the town centre?	Wann fährt der nächste Bus zum Stadtzentrum? *vun fairt dair nekh-ste boos tsoom shtut-tsen-troom*
What is the fare to the airport?	Was kostet die Fahrt zum Flughafen? *vus kos-tet dee fart tsoom flook-hah-fen*
Where is the nearest bus stop?	Wo ist die nächste Bushaltestelle? *vo ist dee nekh-ste boos-hul-te-shtel-le*
Is this the bus stop for...?	Ist das die Haltestelle für den Bus in Richtung...? *ist dus dee hul-te-shtel-le fewr dain boos in rikh-toong*
Does the number 4 stop here?	Hält der Bus Nummer 4 hier an? *helt dair boos noom-mer feer heer un*
Where can I buy a ticket?	Wo kann ich einen Fahrschein kaufen? *vo kunn ikh ine-nen far-shine kow-fen*
Can I pay on the bus?	Kann ich im Bus zahlen? *kunn ikh im boos tsah-len*
Which buses go to the city centre?	Welche Busse fahren ins Stadtzentrum? *vel-khe boos-se fah-ren ins shtut-tsen-troom*

der Bus
dair boos
bus

die Bushaltestelle
dee boos-hul-te-shtel-le
bus station

TAXIS

Where can I get a taxi?	Wo kann ich ein Taxi nehmen? *vo kunn ikh ine tuck-see nay-men*
Can I order a taxi?	Kann ich ein Taxi bestellen? *kunn ikh ine tuck-see be-stel-len*
Can you take me to the library?	Könnten Sie mich zur Bibliothek fahren? *kurn-ten zee mikh tsoor bib-lee-o-tayk fah-ren*
Is it far?	Ist es weit weg? *ist es vyte vek*
How long will it take?	Wie lange wird es dauern? *vee lan-ge veert es dow-ern*
How much will it cost?	Was kostet die Fahrt? *vus kos-tet dee fart*
Can you drop me here?	Können sie mich hier absetzen? *kur-nen zee mikh heer up-zet-sen*
What do I owe you?	Was schulde ich Ihnen? *vus shool-de ikh een-en*
I don't have any change	Ich habe kein Kleingeld *ikh ha-be kine kline-gelt*
Please can I have a receipt?	Kann ich bitte eine Quittung haben? *kunn ikh bi-te ine-e kvit-toong hah-ben*

das Taxi
dus tuck-see
taxi

BOATS

Are there any boat trips?	Gibt es Schifffahrten? *gee-pt es shif-far-ten*
Where does the boat leave from?	Wo fährt das Schiff ab? *vo fairt dus shif up*
When is...	Wann fährt...? *vun fairt*
...the next boat to...?	...das nächste Schiff nach...? *dus nekh-ste shif nakh*
...the first boat?	...das erste Schiff? *dus airs-te shif*
...the last boat?	...das letzte Schiff? *dus lets-te shif*
I'd like two tickets for...	Ich möchte zwei Fahrkarten für... *ikh murkh-te tsvy far-kar-ten fewr*
...the cruise	...die Rundfahrt *dee roont-fart*

die Fähre
dee fai-re
ferry

das Tragflügelboot
dus truk-flew-gel-boht
hydrofoil

die Jacht
dee yakht
yacht

das Hovercraft
dus hover-kraft
hovercraft

...the river trip	...die Flussfahrt *dee floos-fart*
How much is it for...	Was kostet es für...? *vus kos-tet es fewr*
...a car and two people?	...ein Auto und zwei Passagiere? *ine ow-toe oont tsvy passa-sheer-e*
...a family?	...eine Familie? *ine-e fa-mee-lee-ye*
...a cabin?	...eine Kabine? *ine-e kah-bee-ne*
Can I buy a ticket on board?	Kann ich eine Fahrkarte an Bord kaufen? *kunn ikh ine-e far-kar-te un bort kow-fen*
Is there wheelchair access?	Gibt es Zugang für Rollstuhlfahrer? *geept es tsoo-gung fewr roll-shtool-fah-rer*

die Schwimmweste
dee shvim-ves-te
life jacket

der Rettungsring
dair ret-toongs-ring
lifebuoy

der Katamaran
dair ka-ta-ma-run
catamaran

das Ausflugsschiff
dus ows-flewks-shif
pleasure boat

AIR TRAVEL

Which terminal do I need?	Welches ist mein Terminal? *vel-khes ist mine tair-mi-nal*
What time do I check in?	Wann ist der Check-in? *van ist dair check-in*
Where is...	Wo ist... *vo ist*
...the arrivals hall?	...die Ankunftshalle? *dee un-koonfts-hull-le*
...the departures hall?	...die Abflughalle? *dee up-flook-hull-le*
...the boarding gate?	...das Gate? *dus gate*
Where do I check in?	Wo muss ich einchecken? *vo moos ikh ine-check-en*
I'm travelling...	Ich reise in... *ikh rye-ze in*
...economy	...der Economy-Class *dair economy class*
...business class	...der Business Class *dair business class*
Here is my passport	Hier ist mein Pass *heer ist mine pahs*

die Reisetasche
dee ry-ze-tu-she
holdall

die Bordmahlzeit
dee bort-mahl-tsyt
flight meal

der Pass
dair pahs
passport

die Bordkarte
dee bort-kar-te
boarding pass

I have an e-ticket	Ich habe ein E-Ticket *ikh hah-be ine ee-ticket*
I'm checking in one suitcase	Ich checke einen Koffer ein *ikh chek-ke ine-nen kof-fer ine*
I packed it myself	Ich habe ihn selbst gepackt *ikh hah-be een zelpst ge-pukt*
I have one piece of hand luggage	Ich habe ein Stück Handgepäck *ikh hah-be ine shtewk hunt-ge-pek*
What is the weight allowance?	Was ist mein Freigepäck? *vus ist mine fry-ge-pek*
How much is excess baggage?	Was kostet das Übergepäck? *vus kos-tet das ew-ber-ge-pek*
I'd like…	Ich hätte gern… *ikh het-te gairn*
…a window seat	…einen Fensterplatz *ine-nen fen-ster-pluts*
…an aisle seat	…einen Gangplatz *ine-nen gung-pluts*
…a bulk head seat	…einen Bulkhead Seat *ine-nen bulk-head seat*

You may hear …

- **Ihren Pass/Ihren Flugschein, bitte**
  ee-ren pahs/ee-ren flook-shine bit-te
  Your passport/ticket, please

- **Ist das ihre Tasche?**
  ist dus ee-re tu-she
  Is this your bag?

AT THE AIRPORT

Here's my...	Hier ist... *heer ist*
...boarding pass	...meine Bordkarte *my-ne bort-kar-te*
...passport	...mein Pass *mine pahs*
Can I change some money?	Kann ich Geld wechseln? *kunn ikh gelt vek-zeln*

der Reisescheck
dair ry-ze-shek
traveller's cheque

die Passkontrolle
dee pahs-kon-troll-le
passport control

What is the exchange rate?	Wie ist der Wechselkurs? *vee ist dair vek-sel-koors*
Is the flight delayed?	Hat der Flug Verspätung? *hut dair flook fair-shpay-toong*
How late is it?	Wie spät ist es? *vee shpayt ist es*
Which gate does flight... leave from?	Von welchem Gate geht der Flug...ab? *fon vel-khem gate gayt dair flook...up*
What time do I board?	Wann gehe ich an Bord? *vunn gay-e ikh un bort*
When does the gate close?	Wann schließt das Gate? *vun shleest dus gate*
Where are the trolleys?	Wo sind die Trolleys? *vo zint dee trol-leys*

Here is the reclaim tag	Hier ist das Gepäcketikett *heer ist dus ge-pek-eti-ket*
I can't find my baggage	Ich kann mein Gepäck nicht finden *ikh kunn mine ge-pek nikht fin-den*
My baggage hasn't arrived	Mein Gepäck ist nicht angekommen *mine ge-pek ist nikht un-ge-kom-men*

der Duty-Free-Shop
dair duty-free-shop
duty-free shop

der Pilot
dair pee-loht
pilot

die Flugbegleiterin
dee flook-be-gly-tair-in
air stewardess

das Flugzeug
dus flook-tsoyk
aeroplane

der Check-In-Schalter
dair check-in-shul-ter
check-in desk

die Gepäckausgabe
dee ge-pek-ows-gah-be
baggage reclaim

EATING OUT

Germany, Austrian and Swiss food tends to be
hearty and appetizing. You can choose from cafés
and bars (*Weinstube*), which serve a variety of
drinks and snacks, as well as traditional restaurants
(*Gasthöfe*) serving local specialities, and larger
more international eateries (*Gaststätte*). German
beer is especially delicious and justly famous,
and every area has its own special brew, which
you can sample in *Bierkeller* and *Biergärten*.

MAKING A RESERVATION

I'd like...	Ich möchte... *ikh murkh-te*
...to book a table for lunch/dinner	...einen Tisch für heute Mittag/Abend reservieren *ine-nen tish fewr hoy-te mit-tahk/ah-bent re-zair-vee-ren*
...to book a table for four people	...einen Tisch für vier Personen reservieren *ine-nen tish fewr feer per-zoe-nen re-zair-vee-ren*
...to book a table for this evening	...einen Tisch für heute Abend reservieren *ine-nen tish fewr hoy-te ah-bent re-zair-vee-ren*
...to book a table for tomorrow at one	...einen Tisch für morgen dreizehn Uhr reservieren *ine-nen tish fewr mor-gen dry-tsayn oor re-zair-vee-ren*
Do you have a table earlier/later?	Haben Sie einen Tisch früher/später? *hah-ben zee ine-nen tish frew-er/shpay-ter*
My name is...	Mein Name ist... *mine nah-me ist*
My telephone number is...	Meine Telefonnummer ist... *my-ne tay-lay-foen-noom-mer ist*
Do you take credit cards?	Nehmen Sie Kreditkarten? *nay-men zee kray-deet-kar-ten*
I have a reservation	Ich habe eine Reservierung *ikh hah-be ine-e re-zair-vee-roong*
in the name of...	auf den Namen... *owf dain nah-men*
We haven't booked	Wir haben nicht reserviert *veer hah-ben nikht re-zair-veert*

ORDERING A MEAL

Can we see the menu?	Können wir die Speisekarte sehen? *kur-nen veer dee shpy-ze-kar-te zay-hen*
...see the wine list?	...die Weinkarte sehen? *dee vine-kar-te zay-hen*
Do you have...	Haben Sie... *hah-ben zee*
...a set menu?	...ein Mittagsmenü? *ine mit-tahks-menew*
...a fixed-price menu?	...ein Festpreismenü? *ine fest-prize-menew*
...a children's menu?	...ein Kindermenü? *ine kin-der-menew*
...an à la carte menu	...ein Menü à la carte? *ine menew à la carte*
What are today's specials?	Welche Spezialgerichte gibt es heute? *vel-khe shpay-tsee-al-ge-rikhte geept es hoy-te*
What are the local specialities?	Was sind die örtlichen Spezialitäten? *vus zint dee urt-likhen shpay-tsee-al-ee-tay-ten*

You may hear...

- **Haben Sie reserviert?**
  hah-ben zee re-zair-veert
  Do you have a reservation?

- **Auf welchen Namen?**
  owf vel-khen nah-men
  In what name?

- **Bitte nehmen Sie Platz.**
  bit-te nay-men zee pluts
  Please be seated.

- **Möchten Sie bestellen?**
  murkh-ten zee be-shtel-len
  Are you ready to order?

What do you recommend?	Was empfehlen Sie? *vus em-pfay-len zee*
What is this?	Was ist das? *vus ist dus*
Are there any vegetarian dishes?	Haben Sie vegetarische Speisen? *hah-ben zee vay-ge-tah-ree-shuh shpy-zen*
I can't …	Ich kann… *ikh kunn*
…eat dairy foods	…keine Molkereiprodukte essen *kine-e mol-ker-eye-pro-dook-te es-sen*
…eat nuts	…keine Nüsse essen *kine-e news-se es-sen*
…eat wheat	…keinen Weizen essen *kine-nen vy-tsen es-sen*
To start, I'll have…	Als Vorspeise nehme ich… *uls for-shpy-ze nay-me ikh*
To drink, I'll have…	Zum Trinken nehme ich… *tsoom trin-ken nay-me ikh*

Reading the menu

• **Vorspeisen** *for-shpy-zen*	Starters
• **erster Gang** *air-ster gang*	First courses
• **die Hauptspeisen** *dee howpt-shpy-zen*	Main courses
• **das Gemüse** *dus ge-mew-ze*	Vegetables
• **Käse** *kay-ze*	Cheeses
• **die Nachspeisen** *dee nakh-shpy-zen*	Desserts

COMPLAINING

I didn't order this	Das habe ich nicht bestellt *dus hah-be ikh nikht be-shtelt*
We can't wait any longer	Wir können nicht länger warten *veer kur-nen nikht len-ger var-ten*

PAYING

The bill, please	Die Rechnung, bitte *dee rekh-noong bit-te*
Can we pay separately?	Können wir getrennt zahlen? *kur-nen veer ge-trennt tsah-len*
Can I...	Kann ich... *kunn ikh*
...have a receipt?	...eine Quittung haben? *ine-e kvit-toong hah-ben*
...have an itemized bill?	...eine detaillierte Rechnung haben? *ine-e day-ty-leer-te rekh-noong hah-ben*
Is service included?	Ist die Bedienung inbegriffen? *ist dee be-dee-noong in-be-griffen*

You may hear...

- Wir nehmen keine
  Kreditkarten.
  *veer nay-men ky-ne
  kray-deet-kar-ten*
  We don't take credit cards.

- Geben Sie bitte Ihre
  Geheimzahl ein.
  *gay-ben zee bit-te ee-re
  ge-hime-tsahl ine*
  Please enter your PIN.

CROCKERY AND CUTLERY

der Salatteller
dair zah-laht-teller
side plate

die Schüssel
dee shew-sel
bowl

das Salz
dus zults
salt

der Pfeffer
dair pfeffer
pepper

die Tasse und die Untertasse
dee tuss-e oont dee unter-tuss-e
cup and saucer

der Kaffeelöffel
dair kuf-fay-lurfel
teaspoon

das Glas
dus glahs
glass

der Dessertlöffel
dair des-sair-lurfel
dessertspoon

das Messer
dus mes-ser
knife

die Serviette
dee zair-vee-et-te
napkin

die Gabel
dee gah-bel
fork

der Teller
dair tel-ler
dinner plate

AT THE CAFÉ OR BAR

The menu, please	Die Speisekarte, bitte *dee shpy-ze-kar-te bit-te*
Do you have...?	Haben Sie... ? *hah-ben zee*
What fruit juices/herb teas do you have?	Welche Fruchtsäfte/ Kräutertees haben Sie? *vel-khe frookht-zef-te/ kroy-ter-tays hah-ben zee*
I'd like...	Ich möchte... *ikh murkh-te*
I'll have...	Ich nehme... *ikh nay-me*

der Kaffee mit Milch
dair kuf-fay mit milkh
coffee with milk

der schwarze Kaffee
dair shvur-tse kuf-fay
black coffee

der Kaffee mit Schlagsahne
dair kuf-fay mit shluk-zah-ne
coffee with whipped cream

You may hear...

- **Was darf es sein?**
  vus darf es zine
  What would you like?

- **Möchten Sie noch etwas?**
  murkh-ten zee nokh et-vus
  Anything else?

- **Gern geschehen.**
  gairn ge-shay-en
  You're welcome.

der Tee mit Milch
dair tay mit milkh
tea with milk

der Tee mit Zitrone
dair tay mit tsee-troh-ne
tea with lemon

der Pfefferminztee
dair pfef-fer-mints-tay
mint tea

der grüne Tee
dair grew-ne tay
green tea

der Kamillentee
dair kah-mill-len-tay
camomile tea

die heiße Schokolade
dee hy-se shoko-lah-de
hot chocolate

A bottle of…	Eine Flasche… *ine-e flu-shuh*
A glass of…	Ein Glas… *ine glahs*
A cup of…	Eine Tasse… *ine-e tuss-se*
with lemon/milk	…mit Zitrone/Milch *mit tsee-troh-ne/milkh*
Another…please	Noch ein/eine…bitte *nokh ine/ine-e…bit-te*
The same again, please	Bitte das gleiche noch einmal *bit-te dus gly-khe nokh ine-mul*

CAFÉ AND BAR DRINKS

der Eiskaffee
dair ice-kuf-fay
iced coffee

der Orangensaft
dair oh-run-dshen-zuft
fresh orange juice

der Apfelsaft
dair up-fel-zuft
apple juice

der Ananassaft
dair ah-nah-nus-zuft
pineapple juice

der Tomatensaft
dair tomah-ten-zuft
tomato juice

der Traubensaft
dair trow-ben-zuft
grape juice

die Limonade
dee lee-mo-nahde
lemonade

die Apfelschorle
dee up-fel-shorle
sparkling apple juice

die Cola
dee koh-lah
cola

die Flasche Mineralwasser
dee flu-shuh mee-nair-al-vusser
bottle of mineral water

das Sodawasser
dus zo-da-vuss-ser
soda water

die Flasche Bier
dee flu-shuh beer
bottle of beer

das Glas Bier
dus glahs beer
glass of beer

das Glas Rotwein
dus glahs roht-vine
glass of red wine

die Flasche Weißwein
dee flu-shuh vice-vine
bottle of white wine

der Gin und Tonic
dair gin oont tonic
gin and tonic

You may hear...

- **In der Flasche oder vom Fass?**
  in dair flu-shuh odair fom fuss
  Bottled or draught?

- **Mit oder ohne Kohlensäure?**
  mit odair oh-ne ko-len-zoyre
  Still or sparkling?

- **Mit Eis?**
  mit ice
  With ice?

BAR SNACKS

das Sandwich
dus zand-wich
sandwich

die Frankfurter mit Senf
dee frunk-foor-ter mit zenf
Frankfurters with mustard

die Bratwurst mit Kartoffeln
dee brat-voorst mit kar-toffeln
sausages with potatoes

die Currywurst
dee kurry-voorst
curried sausage

der Kartoffelsalat
dair kahr-toffel-zah-laht
potato salad

die Nüsse
dee newss-se
nuts

die Brezeln
dee bray-tseln
pretzels

das Plundergebäck
dus ploon-der-gebek
Danish pastry

der Kuchen
dair koo-khen
cake

das Eis
dus ice
ice cream

FAST FOOD

Can I have...	Kann ich... *kunn ikh*
...to eat in/take away	...hier essen/mitnehmen? *heer ess-sen/mit-nay-men*
...some ketchup/mustard	...etwas Ketchup/Senf haben? *et-vus ketch-up/zenf hah-ben*

der Hamburger
dair ham-burger
hamburger

der Chickenburger
dair chicken-burger
chicken burger

der Wrap
dair rap
wrap

der Hot Dog
dair hot dog
hot dog

der Kebab
dair keh-bub
kebab

die Pommes
dee pomm-mes
French fries

das Brathähnchen
dus braht-hen-khen
fried chicken

die Pizza
dee peetsa
pizza

BREAKFAST

Can I...	Kann ich... *kunn ikh*
...have some sugar	...etwas Zucker haben? *et-vus tsoo-ker hah-ben*
...have some milk	...etwas Milch haben? *et-vus milkh hah-ben*
...have some artificial sweetener	...etwas Süßstoff haben? *et-vus zews-shtoff hah-ben*
...have some butter	...etwas Butter haben? *et-vus boo-ter hah-ben*
...have some jam?	...etwas Marmelade haben? *et-vus mar-meh-lah-de hah-ben*

der Kaffee
dair kuf-fay
coffee

der Tee
dair tay
tea

die heiße Schokolade
dee hy-se shoko-lah-de
hot chocolate

der Orangensaft
dair oh-run-dshen-zuft
orange juice

der Apfelsaft
dair up-fel-zuft
apple juice

das Brot
dus broht
bread

das Brötchen
dus brurt-khen
bread roll

das Croissant
dus krwassant
croissant

der Honig
dair hoh-nik
honey

das Rührei
dus ruhr-eye
scrambled eggs

das gekochte Ei
dus ge-kokh-te eye
boiled egg

das pochierte Ei
dus posheer-te eye
poached egg

das frische Obst
dus free-shuh opst
fresh fruit

der Fruchtjoghurt
dair frewkht-yog-hurt
fruit yoghurt

der Schinken
dair shin-ken
ham

der Käse
dair kay-ze
cheese

FIRST COURSES

die Suppe
dee zoop-pe
soup

die Fleischbrühe
dee flysh-brew-e
broth

die Brotsuppe
dee broht-zoop-pe
bread soup

die Rindersuppe
dee rinder-zoop-pe
beef broth

der Borscht
dair borsht
beetroot soup

die Kartoffelsuppe
dee kar-toffel-zoop-pe
potato soup

die Fritattensuppe
dee frit-tah-ten-zoop-pe
broth with pancake strips

das Soufflé
dus zoof-lay
soufflé

das Omelett
dus om-lett
omelette

die Eierspeise
dee eye-er-shpy-ze
scrambled omelette

der Eier und Pilzsalat
dair eye-er oont pilts-zah-laht
egg and mushroom salat

die Forelle mit Spargel
dee for-rell-le mit shpar-gel
trout withasparagus

der Räucherlachs
dair roy-kher-lukhs
smoked salmon

der Heringsalat
dair hair-ring-zah-laht
pickled herring salad

die gegrillten Garnelen
dee ge-grill-ten gar-nay-len
grilled prawns

der Räucherschinken
dair roy-kher-shin-ken
cured ham

der Aufschnitt
dair owf-shnit
cold meats

die gefüllte Tomate
dee ge-fewl-te toh-mah-te
stuffed tomato

das gefüllte Gemüse
dus ge-fewl-te ge-mew-ze
stuffed vegetables

die Pilze in Aspik
dee pil-tse in us-peek
mushrooms in aspic

MAIN COURSES

I would like...	Ich möchte... *ikh murkh-te*
...the chicken	...das Hähnchen *dus hen-khen*
...the duck	...die Ente *dee en-te*
...the lamb	...das Lamm *dus lum*
...the pork	...das Schweinefleisch *dus shvy-ne-flysh*
...the beef	...das Rindfleisch *dus rind-flysh*
...the steak	...das Beefsteak *dus beef-steak*
...the veal	...das Kalbfleisch *dus kulp-flysh*
...the liver	...die Leber *dee lay-ber*
roast	gebraten *ge-brah-ten*
baked	gebacken *ge-buck-en*
grilled	gegrillt *ge-grillt*
on skewers	am Spieß *um shpees*

You may see...

die Meeresfrüchte
dee mair-es-frewkh-te
seafood

die Fische
dee fishe
fish

You may hear...

• **Wie möchten Sie Ihr Steak?**
vee murkh-ten zee eer steak
How do you like your steak?

• **Englisch, medium oder durchgebraten?**
eng-lish, mee-dee-um oh-dair doorkh-ge-brah-ten
Rare, medium or well done?

barbecued	gegrillt *ge-grillt*
poached	pochiert *po-sheert*
boiled	gekocht *ge-kokht*
fried	gebraten *ge-brah-ten*
pan-fried/sautéed	kurzgebraten *koorts-ge-brah-ten*
stuffed	gefüllt *ge-fewllt*
stewed	gegart *ge-gart*
with cheese	mit Käse *mit kay-ze*

das Geflügel
dus ge-flew-gel
poultry

das Fleisch
dus flysh
meat

SALADS AND SIDE DISHES

das Kartoffelpüree
dus kar-toffel-pew-reh
creamed potato

gedünstete Gemüse
ge-dewns-te-te ge-mew-ze
steamed vegetables

der grüne Salat
dair grew-ne zah-laht
green salad

der gemischte Salat
dair ge-mish-te zah-laht
mixed salad

die Nudeln
dee noo-deln
pasta

der Reis
dair rice
rice

der Spinat
dair shpee-naht
spinach

die Pommes
dee pom-mes
chips

der Rotkohl
dair roht-kohl
red cabbage

das Sauerkraut
dus zower-krowt
sauerkraut

DESSERTS

der Schokoladenpudding
dair shoko-lah-den-poo-ding
chocolate pudding

die Pfannkuchen
dee pfunn-koo-khen
pancakes

der Apfelstrudel
dair up-fel-shtroo-del
apple strudel

die Quarkknödel
dee kvark-knur-del
curd cheese dumplings

der Sorbet
dair zor-bay
sorbet

das Speiseeis
dus shpy-ze-ice
ice cream

die Rote Grütze
dee roh-te grewt-tse
mixed berry compote

der Kuchen
dair koo-khen
cake

Berliner mit Mousse
bair-lee-ner mit moos
doughnuts with mousse

der Zwetschgendatschi
dair tsvetsh-gen-daht-shee
Bavarian plum tart

PLACES TO STAY

Germany, Austria and Switzerland have a wide range of places to stay, depending on your personal preference and budget. These range from elegant city hotels and historic *Schlösser* to smaller, family-run *Pensionen* and traditional *Gasthöfe* (country inns). If you prefer self-catering, you can rent a chalet or apartment, or find a campsite to park your caravan or put up your tent.

MAKING A RESERVATION

I'd like...	Ich möchte gern... *ikh murkh-te gairn*
...to make a reservation	...ein Zimmer reservieren *ine tsim-mer re-zair-veer-en*
...a double room	...ein Doppelzimmer *ine dop-pel-tsim-mer*
...a twin-bedded room	...ein Zweibettzimmer *ine tsvy-bet-tsim-mer*
...a single room	...ein Einzelzimmer *ine ine-tsel-tsim-mer*
...a family room	...ein Familienzimmer *ine fa-meelee-yen-tsim-mer*
...a disabled person's room	...ein Behindertenzimmer *ine be-hin-dair-ten-tsim-mer*
...with a bath/shower	...mit Bad/Dusche *mit baht/doo-she*
...with a sea view	...mit Blick aufs Meer *mit blik owfs mair*
...with a balcony	...mit Balkon *mit bul-kong*
...for two nights	...für zwei Nächte *fewr tsvy nekh-te*
...for a week	...für eine Woche *fewr ine-e vo-khe*
...from...to...	...vom...bis *fom...bis*
Is breakfast included?	Ist das Frühstück inbegriffen? *ist dus frew-shtewk in-be-griffen*
How much is it...	Wie viel kostet es... *vee feel kos-tet es*
...per night?	...pro Nacht? *pro nakht*
...per week?	...pro Woche? *pro vo-khe*

CHECKING IN

I have a reservation in the name of...	Ich habe eine Reservierung auf den Namen... *ikh hah-be ine-e re-zair-vee-rung owf dain nah-men*
Do you have...	Haben Sie...? *hah-ben zee*

ein Gepäckträger
ine ge-pek-trayger
a porter

die Lifte
dee lif-te
lifts

der Zimmerservice
dair tsim-mer-service
room service

die Minibar
dee mini-bar
mini bar

I'd like...	Ich hätte gern... *ikh het-te gairn*
...the keys for room...	...die Schlüssel zum Zimmer... *dee shlew-sel tsoom tsim-mer*
...a wake-up call at...	...einen Weckruf um... *ine-nen vek-roof oom*
What time is...	Um wie viel Uhr ist... *oom vee feel oor ist*
...breakfast?	...das Frühstück? *dus frew-shtewk*
...dinner?	...das Abendessen? *dus ah-bent-es-sen*

IN YOUR ROOM

Do you have...	**Haben Sie...** *hah-ben zee*
another...	**ein anderes...** *ine un-dair-es*
some more...	**noch mehr...** *nokh mair*

die Kopfkissen
dee kopf-kis-sen
pillows

die Decken
dee dek-ken
blankets

eine Glühbirne
ine-e glew-beer-ne
a light bulb

einen Adapter
ine-nen ah-dup-tair
an adapter

You may hear...

- **Ihre Zimmernummer ist...**
eere tsim-mer-noom-mer ist
Your room number is...

- **Hier ist Ihr Schlüssel.**
heer ist eer shlew-sel
Here is your key.

IN THE HOTEL

The room is...	Das Zimmer ist... *dus tsim-mer ist*
...too hot	...zu warm *tsoo varm*
...too cold	...zu kalt *tsoo kult*
...too small	...zu klein *tsoo kline*

der Thermostat
dair tair-mo-stat
thermostat

der Heizkörper
dair hyts-kur-per
radiator

das Einzelzimmer
dus ine-tsel-tsim-mer
single room

das Doppelzimmer
dus dop-pel-tsim-mer
double room

die Zimmernummer
dee tsim-mer-noom-mer
room number

der Wasserkocher
dair vus-ser-ko-kher
kettle

The window won't open	Das Fenster lässt sich nicht öffnen *dus fens-ter lest sikh nikht urf-nen*
The TV doesn't work	Der Fernseher funktioniert nicht *dair fairn-zay-er foonk-tsee-yoneert nikht*

der Kleiderbügel
dair kly-der-bew-gel
coat hanger

der Fernseher
dair fairn-zay-er
television

die Jalousie
dee sha-loo-zee
venetian blind

die Fernbedienung
dee fairn-be-dee-nung
remote control

CHECKING OUT

When do I have to vacate the room?	Wann muss ich das Zimmer freimachen? *van moos ikh dus tsim-mer fry-ma-khen*
Can I have the bill, please.	Kann ich bitte die Rechnung haben? *kunn ikh bit-te dee rekh-noong hah-ben*
Can I pay...	Kann ich... *kunn ikh*
...by credit card?	...mit Kreditkarte zahlen? *mit kray-deet-kar-te tsah-len*
...cash?	...bar zahlen? *bar tsah-len*
I'd like a receipt	Ich hätte gern eine Quittung *ikh het-te gairn ine-e kvit-toong*

IN THE BATHROOM

die Badewanne
dee bah-de-van-ne
bathtub

das Bidet
dus bee-day
bidet

die Seife
dee zy-fe
soap

die Handtücher
dee hunt-tewkher
towels

der Bademantel
dair bah-de-mun-tel
bathrobe

das Schaumbad
dus showm-baht
bubblebath

das Duschgel
dus doosh-gel
shower gel

das Deodorant
dus deo-do-runt
deodorant

die Körperlotion
dee kur-per-lo-tsee-on
body lotion

die Zahnpasta
dee tsahn-pasta
toothpaste

die Zahnbürste
dee tsahn-bewrste
toothbrush

die Mundspülung
dee moont-shpewloong
mouthwash

der Rasierapparat
dair rahzeer-uppurat
electric razor

der Rasierschaum
dair rahzeer-showm
shaving foam

das Rasiermesser
dus rahzeer-mes-ser
razor

der Föhn
dair furn
hairdryer

das Shampoo
dus sham-poo
shampoo

die Pflegespülung
dee pfle-ge-shpewloong
conditioner

die Nagelschere
dee nah-gel-shair-re
nail clippers

die Nagelzange
dee nah-gel-tsan-ge
nail scissors

SELF-CATERING

Can we please...	Könnten wir bitte... *kurn-ten veer bit-te*
...have the key?	...den Schlüssel haben? *dain shlew-sel hah-ben*
...have an extra bed?	...ein Extrabett haben? *ine extra-bet hah-ben*
...have a child's bed?	...ein Kinderbett haben? *ine kin-der-bet hah-ben*

der Hochstuhl *dair hokh-shtool* high chair	**das Gitterbettchen** *dus gitter-bet-khen* cot

...have more cutlery/crockery	...mehr Besteck/Geschirr haben? *mair be-shtek/ge-sheer hah-ben*
Where is...	Wo ist... *vo ist*
...the fusebox?	...der Sicherungskasten? *dair zi-kher-oongs-kus-ten*
...the stopcock?	...der Absperrhahn? *dair up-shpair-hahn*
...the nearest doctor?	...der nächste Arzt? *dair nekh-ste artst*
...the supermarket?	...der Supermarkt? *dair zoo-per-markt*
...the nearest shop?	...der nächste Laden? *dair nekh-ste lah-den*
Do you do babysitting?	Bieten Sie Babysitting? *bee-ten zee baby-sitting*

Is there...	Gibt es eine...
	geept es ine-e
...air conditioning?	...Klimaanlage?
	klee-ma-un-lah-ge
...central heating?	...Zentralheizung?
	tsen-tral-hy-tsoong
How does the heating work?	Wie funktioniert die Heizung?
	vee foonk-tsee-yoneert dee hy-tsoong

der Ventilator
dair ven-tee-la-tor
fan

der Heizlüfter
dair hyts-lewf-tair
convector heater

When does the cleaner come?	Wann kommt die Putzfrau?
	vun kommt dee poots-frow
Where do I put the rubbish?	Wo kommt der Müll hin?
	vo kommt dair mewl hin
Who do we contact if there are problems?	An wen wende ich mich bei Problemen?
	un vain ven-de ikh mikh by pro-blay-men
Do you take pets?	Sind Haustiere erlaubt?
	zint hows-teere air-lowpt

der Hund
dair hoont
dog

IN THE VILLA

Is there an inventory?	Gibt es eine Inventarliste? *geept es ine-e in-ven-tar-lee-ste*
Where is this item?	Wo ist dieser Artikel? *vo ist dee-zer ar-tee-kel*
I need...	Ich brauche... *ikh brow-khe*
...an adapter	...einen Adapter *ine-nen ah-dup-ter*
...an extension lead	...ein Verlängerungskabel *ine fer-len-ger-oongs-kah-bel*
...a torch	...eine Taschenlampe *ine-e tush-en-lum-pe*

der Mikrowellenherd
dair mee-kro-vell-len-hairt
microwave

das Bügeleisen
dus bew-gel-eye-zen
iron

das Bügelbrett
dus bew-gel-bret
ironing board

der Wischmopp und Eimer
dair vish-mop oont eye-mer
mop and bucket

das Kehrblech/der Handbesen
dus kair-blekh/dair hunt-bay-zen
dust pan/brush

das Waschpulver
dus vush-pool-fer
detergent

PROBLEM SOLVING

The shower doesn't work	Die Dusche funktioniert nicht *dee doo-she foonk-tsee-yoneert nikht*
Can you mend it today?	Können Sie das heute reparieren? *kurn-nen zee dus hoy-te re-pah-ree-ren*
There's…	Es gibt… *es geept*
…no electricity	…keinen Strom *kine-nen shtrom*
…no water	…kein Wasser *kine vus-ser*

die Waschmaschine
dee vush-mah-shee-ne
washing machine

der Gefrierkühlschrank
dair ge-freer-kewl-shrunk
fridge-freezer

der Mülleimer
dair mewl-eye-mer
rubbish bin

das Schloss und der Schlüssel
dus shlos oont dair shlew-sel
lock and key

der Rauchmelder
dair rowkh-melder
smoke alarm

der Feuerlöscher
dair foy-er-lursher
fire extinguisher

KITCHEN EQUIPMENT

der Dosenöffner
dair doh-zen-urf-ner
can opener

der Flaschenöffner
dair flu-shen-urf-ner
bottle opener

der Korkenzieher
dair kor-ken-tsee-her
corkscrew

das Hackbrett
dus huk-bret
chopping board

das Küchenmesser
dus kew-khen-mes-ser
kitchen knife

der Gemüseschäler
dair ge-mew-ze-shay-ler
peeler

der Rührbesen
dair rewr-bay-zen
whisk

der Kochlöffel
dair kokh-lurfel
wooden spoon

der Schaber
dair shah-ber
spatula

das Reibeisen
dus ribe-eye-zen
grater

das Sieb
dus zeeb
colander

die Bratpfanne
dee brut-pfan-ne
frying pan

der Stieltopf
dair shteel-topf
saucepan

die Grillpfanne
dee grill-pfan-ne
grill pan

der Schmortopf
dair shmor-topf
casserole dish

die Rührschüssel
dee rewr-shew-sel
mixing bowl

der Mixer
dair mixer
blender

das Backblech
dus buk-blekh
baking tray

der Topflappen
dair topf-lappen
oven gloves

die Schürze
dee shewr-tse
apron

CAMPING

Where is the nearest...	Wo ist der nächste... *vo ist dair nekh-ste*
...campsite?	...Campingplatz? *kam-ping-pluts*
...caravan site?	...Wohnwagenplatz? *vohn-vah-gen-pluts*
Do you have any vacancies?	Sind hier Plätze frei? *zint heer plet-se fry*
What is the charge...	Wie viel kostet es... *vee-feel kos-tet es*
...per night?	...pro Nacht? *pro nakht*
...per week?	...pro Woche? *pro vo-khe*
Does the price...	Ist im Preis... *ist im prize*
...include electricity?	...der Strom inbegriffen? *dair shtrohm in-be-griffen*
...include hot water?	...das warme Wasser inbegriffen? *dus var-me vas-ser in-be-griffen*
We want to stay for...	Wir möchten...Nächte bleiben *veer murkh-ten...nekh-te bly-ben*

der Hering
dair hair-ring
tent peg

das Zelt
dus tselt
tent

die Zeltspannleine
dee tselt-shpun-lye-ne
guy rope

Can I...	Kann ich... *kunn ikh*
...rent a tent?	...ein Zelt mieten? *ine tselt mee-ten*
...rent a bicycle?	...ein Fahrrad mieten? *ine far-raht mee-ten*
...rent a barbecue?	...einen Grill mieten? *ine-nen grill mee-ten*
Where are...	Wo sind... *vo zint*
...the toilets?	...die Toiletten? *dee twah-let-ten*
...the dustbins?	...die Mülltonnen? *dee mewl-ton-nen*
Are there...	Gibt es... *geept es*
...showers?	...Duschen? *doo-shen*
...laundry facilities?	...eine Waschküche? *ine-e vash-kew-khe*
Is there...	Gibt es... *geept es*
...a swimming pool?	...ein Schwimmbad? *ine shvim-baht*
...a shop?	...einen Laden? *ine-nen lah-den*

You may hear...

- **Feuer sind nicht erlaubt.**
  foy-er zint nikht er-lowpt
  Don't light a fire.

- **Das Wasser ist nicht trinkbar.**
  dus vuss-ser ist nikht trink-bar
  Don't drink the water.

AT THE CAMPSITE

die Luftmatratze
dee looft-mah-trat-se
air mattress

der Schlafsack
dair shlaf-zuck
sleeping bag

der Campingkessel
dair kam-ping-kes-sel
camping kettle

der Grill
dair grill
barbecue

der Campingkocher
dair kam-ping-ko-kher
camping stove

die Kühltasche
dee kewl-tush-e
coolbox

das Flaschenwasser
dus flu-shen-vus-ser
bottled water

der Picknickkorb
dair pick-nick-korp
picnic hamper

die Thermosflasche
dee tair-mos-fla-shuh
vacuum flask

der Eimer
dair eye-mer
bucket

das Insektenschutzmittel
dus in-zek-ten-shoots-mittel
insect repellent

das Sonnenschutzmittel
dus zon-nen-shoots-mittel
sunscreen

der Holzhammer
dair holts-ham-mer
mallet

der Kompass
dair kom-puss
compass

das Pflaster
dus pflus-ter
plaster

der Schnurknäuel
dair shnoor-knoy-el
ball of string

die Taschenlampe
dee tu-shen-lum-pe
torch

der Rucksack
dair rook-zuck
backpack

die Wanderstiefel
dee vun-der-shtee-fel
walking boots

die Regenbekleidung
dee ray-gen-be-kly-doong
waterproofs

SHOPPING

As well as department stores, supermarkets and specialist shops, Germany has many picturesque open-air markets in town squares and high streets where you can buy food, clothes and even antiques relatively cheaply. Most shops are open between 9.00am and 6–8.00pm Mondays to Fridays. Note that many close at 4.00pm on Saturdays. Weekly markets (*Wochenmärkte*) are often held on Saturdays in many towns.

IN THE STORE

I'm looking for...	Ich suche nach... *ikh zoo-khe nakh*
Do you have...?	Haben Sie...? *hah-ben zee*
I'm just looking	Ich sehe mich nur um *ikh zay-he mikh noor oom*
I'm being served	Ich werde schon bedient *ikh vair-de shon be-deent*
Do you have any more of these?	Haben Sie noch mehr von diesen? *hah-ben zee nokh mair fon dee-zen*
How much is this?	Wie viel kostet das? *vee feel kos-tet dus*
Have you anything cheaper?	Haben Sie etwas Billigeres? *hah-ben zee et-vus bee-lee-ger-es*
I'll take this one	Ich nehme dieses *ikh nay-me dee-zes*
Where can I pay?	Wo kann ich zahlen? *vo kunn ikh tsah-len*
I'll pay...	Ich zahle... *ikh tsah-le*
...in cash	...bar *bar*
...by credit card	...mit Kreditkarte *mit kray-deet-kar-te*
Can I have a receipt?	Kann ich eine Quittung haben? *kunn ikh ine-e kvit-toong hah-ben*
I'd like to exchange this	Ich möchte das gern umtauschen *ikh murkh-te dus gairn oom-tow-shen*

IN THE BANK

I'd like…	Ich möchte… *ikh murkh-te*
…to make a withdrawal	…Geld abheben *gelt up-hay-ben*
…to pay in some money	…Geld einzahlen *gelt ine-tsah-len*
…to change some money	…Geld wechseln *gelt vek-seln*
…into euros	…in Euro *in oy-roe*
…into sterling	…in britische Pfund *in brit-tishe pfoont*
Here is my passport	Hier ist mein Pass *heer ist mine pahs*
My name is…	Ich heiße… *ikh hys-se*
My account number is…	Meine Kontonummer ist… *my-ne kon-toe-noo-mer ist*
My bank details are…	Meine Bankangaben lauten… *my-ne bunk-un-gah-ben low-ten*

der Wechselkurs
dair vek-sel-koors
exchange rate

der Reisescheck
dair ry-ze-shek
traveller's cheque

der Pass
dair pahs
passport

das Geld
dus gelt
money

Do I have…	Muss ich… *moos ikh*
…to key in my PIN?	…meine Geheimzahl eingeben? *my-ne ge-hime-tsal ine-gay-ben*
…to sign here?	…hier unterschreiben? *heer oon-ter-shry-ben*
Is there a cash machine?	Gibt es einen Geldautomaten? *geept es ine-nen gelt-ow-toe-mah-ten*
Can I withdraw money on my credit card?	Kann ich Geld mit meiner Kreditkarte abheben? *kunn ikh gelt mit my-ner kray-deet-kar-te up-hay-ben*
Can I cash a cheque?	Kann ich einen Scheck einlösen? *kunn ikh ine-nen shek ine-lur-zen*
When does the bank open/close?	Wann öffnet/schließt die Bank? *vun urf-net/shleest dee bunk*

der Geldautomat
dair gelt-ow-toe-maht
cash machine

der Bankdirektor
dair bunk-dee-rek-tor
bank manager

die Kreditkarte
dee kray-deet-kar-te
credit card

das Scheckbuch
dus shek-bookh
chequebook

SHOPS

der Bäcker
dair bek-ker
baker's

der Gemüseladen
dair ge-mew-ze-lahden
greengrocer's

das Delikatessengeschäft
dus deli-kah-tessen-gesheft
delicatessen

der Fischhändler
dair fish-hendler
fishmonger

die Tabaktrafik
dee tah-buk-trahfik
tobacconist

die Boutique
dee booteek
boutique

der Plattengeschäft
dair plu-ten-gesheft
record shop

das Möbelgeschäft
dus mur-bel-gesheft
furniture shop

die Fleischerei
dee fly-shuh-rye
butcher's

die Gemischtwarenhandlung
dee gemisht-vahren-hundloong
grocer's

der Supermarkt
dair zooper-markt
supermarket

die Buchhandlung
dee bookh-hundloong
book shop

das Schuhgeschäft
dus shoo-gesheft
shoe shop

der Schneider
dair shny-der
tailor's

der Juwelier
dair yoo-vay-leer
jeweller's

der Eisenwarenhändler
dair eye-zen-vahren-hendler
hardware shop

AT THE MARKET

I would like…	Ich hätte gern… *ikh het-te gairn*
How much is this?	Wie viel kostet das? *vee-feel kos-tet dus*
What's the price per kilo?	Wie viel kostet ein Kilo? *vee-feel kos-tet ine kee-lo*
It's too expensive	Das ist zu teuer *dus ist tsoo toy-er*
Do you have anything cheaper?	Haben Sie etwas Billigeres? *hah-ben zee et-vus billy-gair-es*
That's fine, I'll take it	Das ist gut, ich nehme es *dus ist goot ikh nay-me es*
I'll take two kilos	Ich nehme zwei Kilo *ikh nay-me tsvy kee-lo*
A kilo of…	Ein Kilo von… *ine kee-lo fon*
Half a kilo of…	Ein Pfund von… *ine pfoont fon*
A little more, please	Bitte etwas mehr *bit-te et-vus mair*
May I taste it?	Kann ich es kosten? *kunn ikh es kos-ten*
That will be all, thank you	Das ist alles, danke *dus ist alles dun-ke*

You may hear...

- **Sie wünschen bitte?**
  zee vewn-shen bit-te
  Can I help you?

- **Wie viel möchten Sie?**
  vee-feel murkh-ten zee
  How much would you like?

IN THE SUPERMARKET

Where is/are...	Wo ist/sind... *vo ist/zint*
...the frozen foods	...die Tiefkühlkost? *dee teef-kewl-kost*
...the drinks aisle?	...der Gang mit den Getränken? *dair gung mit dain ge-tren-ken*

der Einkaufswagen
dair ine-kowfs-vahgen
trolley

der Einkaufskorb
dair ine-kowfs-korp
basket

...the check-out?	...die Kasse? *dee kuss-se*
I'm looking for...	Ich suche nach... *ikh soo-khe nakh*
Do you have any more?	Haben Sie noch mehr davon? *hah-ben zee nokh mair du-fon*
Is this reduced?	Ist das reduziert? *ist dus re-doo-tsiert*
Where do I pay?	Wo kann ich zahlen? *vo kunn ikh tsah-len*
Shall I key in my PIN?	Soll ich meine Geheimzahl eingeben? *zoll ikh my-ne ge-hime-tsal ine-gay-ben*
Can I have a bag?	Kann ich eine Tragtasche haben? *kunn ikh ine-e trahk-tu-she hah-ben*

FRUIT

die Orange
dee o-run-dsche
orange

die Zitrone
dee tsee-troh-ne
lemon

die Limone
dee lee-moh-ne
lime

die Grapefruit
dee grape-fruit
grapefruit

der Pfirsich
dair pfeehr-zikh
peach

die Nektarine
dee nek-tah-ree-ne
nectarine

die Aprikose
dee upri-ko-ze
apricot

die Pflaume
dee pflow-me
plum

die Kirschen
dee keer-shen
cherries

die Blaubeeren
dee blow-beh-ren
blueberries

die Erdbeere
dee airt-beh-re
strawberry

die Himbeere
dee him-beh-re
raspberry

die Melone
dee may-lo-ne
melon

die Weintrauben
dee vine-trow-ben
grapes

die Banane
dee ba-na-ne
banana

der Granatapfel
dair grah-naht-up-fel
pomegranate

der Apfel
dair up-fel
apple

die Birne
dee beer-ne
pear

die Ananas
dee ana-nahs
pineapple

die Mango
dee mun-go
mango

VEGETABLES

die Kartoffel
dee kar-toffel
potato

die Karotten
dee kah-rotten
carrots

die Paprikaschote
dee pap-ree-kah-shoh-te
pepper

die Chillischoten
dee chilli-shoh-ten
chillis

die Aubergine
dee oh-bair-gee-ne
aubergine

die Tomate
dee toh-mah-te
tomato

die Frühlingszwiebel
dee frew-lings-tsvee-bel
spring onion

der Lauch
dair lowkh
leek

die Zwiebel
dee tsvee-bel
onion

der Knoblauch
dair khnop-lowkh
garlic

die Pilze
dee piltse
mushrooms

die Zucchini
dee tsoo-kee-nee
courgette

die Gurke
dee goor-ke
cucumber

die grüne Bohnen
dee grew-ne boh-nen
French beans

die Erbsen
dee airp-zen
garden peas

der Sellerie
dair zell-air-ee
celery

der Spinat
dair shpee-naht
spinach

der Brokkoli
dair bro-ko-lee
broccoli

der Kohl
dair koal
cabbage

der Salat
dair Zah-laht
lettuce

MEAT AND POULTRY

May I...	Kann ich... *kunn ikh*
...have a slice of...?	...eine Scheibe...haben? *ine-e shy-be...hah-ben*
...have a piece of...?	...ein Stück...haben? *ine shtewk...hah-ben*

der Schinken
dair shin-ken
cooked ham

die Zervelatwurst
dee tsair-veh-laht-voorst
cervelat

die Leberwurst
dee lay-ber-voorst
liverwurst

das Hackfleisch
dus huck-flysh
mince

das Steak
dus steak
steak

das Kotelett
dus koht-let
chop

das Hähnchen
dus hen-khen
chicken

die Ente
dee en-te
duck

FISH AND SHELLFISH

die Forelle
dee for-rell-le
trout

der Lachs
dair lahkhs
salmon

der Kabeljau
dair kah-bel-yow
cod

der Seebarsch
dair zay-bursh
sea bass

die Seebrasse
dee zay-brass-se
sea bream

die Makrele
dee muk-ray-le
mackerel

die Krabbe
dee khrub-be
crab

der Hummer
dair hoom-mer
lobster

die Garnele
dee gahr-nay-le
prawn

die Jakobsmuschel
dee yu-kobs-moo-shel
scallop

BREAD AND CAKES

das Weißbrot
dus vice-broht
white bread

das Roggenbrot
dus roggen-broht
rye bread

die Salzstangen
dee zults-shtan-gen
salt sticks

das Brötchen
dus broht-khen
bread roll

die Schokoladentorte
dee shoko-lah-den-tor-t-e
chocolate cake

die Sachertorte
dee zakher-tor-te
Sachertorte

der Guglhupf
dair google-hoopf
Guglhupf

die Schwazwälderkirschtorte
dee shvarts-velder-keersh-tor-te
Black Forest cake

der Käsekuchen
dair kay-ze-koo-khen
cheesecake

der Stollen
dair shtoll-len
stollen

DAIRY PRODUCE

die Vollmilch
dee foll-milkh
whole milk

die Halbfettmilch
dee hulp-fet-milkh
semi-skimmed milk

die Ziegenmilch
dee tsee-gen-milkh
goat's milk

die saure Sahne
dee zow-re zah-ne
sour cream

die Schlagsahne
dee shluk-zah-ne
whipped cream

der Joghurt
dair yog-hurt
yoghurt

die Butter
dee boot-ter
butter

der Ziegenkäse
dair tsee-gen-kay-ze
goat's cheese

der Emmenthaler
dair emmen-tah-ler
Emmenthal

der Greyerzer
dair grey-air-tser
Gruyère

NEWSPAPERS AND MAGAZINES

Do you have...	Haben Sie... *hah-ben zee*
...a book of stamps?	...ein Briefmarkenheft? *ine breef-mar-ken-heft*
...airmail stamps?	...Luftpostmarken? *looft-posst-mar-ken*
...a packet of envelopes?	...eine Packung Briefumschläge? *ine-e puk-koong breef-oom-shlay-ge*
...some sticky tape?	...einen Klebestreifen? *ine-nen klay-be-shtry-fen*

die Ansichtskarte
dee un-zikhts-kar-te
postcard

die Briefmarken
dee breef-mar-ken
stamps

der Bleistift
dair bly-shtift
pencil

der Kugelschreiber
dair koo-gel-shry-ber
pen

You may hear...

- **Wie alt sind Sie?**
  vee ahlt zint zee
  How old are you?

- **Haben Sie einen Ausweis?**
  hah-ben zee ine-nen ows-vice
  Do you have ID?

...a pack of cigarettes	...eine Packung Zigaretten
	ine-e pu-koong
	tsee-gah-ret-ten

...a box of matches	...eine Schachtel Streichhölzer
	ine-e shakh-tel
	shtrike-hurl-tser

der Tabak
dair tah-buk
tobacco

das Feuerzeug
dus foyer-tsoyk
lighter

der Kaugummi
dair kow-goo-mee
chewing gum

die Bonbons
dee bom-bongs
sweets

die Zeitung
dee tsy-toong
newspaper

die Zeitschriften
dee tsyt-shrif-ten
magazines

das Komikheft
dus komic-heft
comic

die Farbstifte
dee farp-shtif-te
colouring pencils

BUYING CLOTHES

I am looking for...	Ich suche... *ikh zoo-khe*
I am size...	Ich bin Größe... *ikh bin grur-se*
Do you have this...	Haben Sie das... *hah-ben zee dus*
...in my size?	...in meiner Größe? *in my-ner grur-se*
...in small	...in klein *in kline*
...in medium?	...in mittlerer Größe? *in mit-ler-er grur-se*
...in large?	...in einer großen Größe? *in ine-er grur-sen grur-se*
...in other colours?	...in anderen Farben? *in un-de-ren far-ben*
Can I try this on?	Kann ich das anprobieren? *kunn ikh dus un-pro-bee-ren*
It's...	Es ist... *es ist*
...too big	...zu groß *tsoo grohs*
...too small	...zu klein *tsoo kline*
I need...	Ich brauche... *ikh brow-khe*
...a larger size	...eine größere Größe *ine-e grur-se-re grur-se*
...a smaller size	...eine kleinere Größe *ine-e kline-er-re grur-se*
I'll take this one, please	Ich nehme das, bitte *ikh nay-me dus bit-te*
Is this on sale?	Ist das im Ausverkauf? *ist dus im ows-fair-kowf*

BUYING SHOES

I take shoe size…	Meine Schuhgröße ist… *my-ne shoo-grur-se ist*
Can I…	Kann ich… *kunn ikh*
…try this pair?	…dieses Paar anprobieren? *dee-zes par un-pro-bee-ren*
…try those ones in the window?	…die in der Auslage anprobieren? *dee in dair ows-lah-ge un-pro-bee-ren*
These are…	Die sind… *dee zint*
…too tight	…zu knapp *tsoo knup*
…too big	…zu groß *tsoo grohs*
…too small	…zu klein *tsoo kline*
…uncomfortable	…nicht bequem *nikht be-kvaym*
Is there a bigger/smaller size?	Haben Sie eine größere/kleinere Größe? *hah-ben zee ine grur-se-re/kline-ne-re grur-se*

Clothes and shoe sizes guide

Women's clothes sizes

UK	6	8	10	12	14	16	18	20
Europe	34	36	38	40	42	44	46	48
USA	4	6	8	10	12	14	16	18

Men's clothes sizes

UK	36	38	40	42	44	46	48	50
Europe	46	48	50	52	54	56	58	60
USA	36	38	40	42	44	46	48	50

Women's shoes

UK	3	4	5	6	7	8	9
Europe	36	37	38	39	40	42	43
USA	5	6	7	8	9	10	11

CLOTHES AND SHOES

das Kleid
dus klite
dress

das Abendkleid
dus ah-bent-klite
evening dress

die Jacke
dee yuk-ke
jacket

der Pullover
dair pull-oh-ver
jumper

die Jeans
dee jeans
jeans

der Rock
dair rock
skirt

die Trainers
dee trainers
trainers

die Stiefeln
dee shtee-feln
boots

die Handtasche
dee hunt-tush-e
handbag

der Gürtel
dair gewr-tel
belt

der Anzug
dair un-tsook
suit

der Mantel
dair mun-tel
coat

das Hemd
dus hemt
shirt

das T-Shirt
dus t-shirt
t-shirt

die Shorts
dee shorts
shorts

die Schuhe mit hohem Absatz
dee shoo-e mit hohem up-zuts
high-heel shoes

die Schnürschuhe
dee shnewr-shoo-e
lace-up shoes

die Sandalen
dee zun-dah-len
sandals

die Flipflops
dee flip-flops
flip-flop

die Socken
dee zok-ken
socks

AT THE GIFT SHOP

I'd like to…	Ich möchte gern… *ikh murkh-te gairn*
…buy a gift for my mother/father	…ein Geschenk für meine Mutter/meinen Vater kaufen *ine geshenk fewr my-ne moo-ter/my-nen fah-ter kow-fen*
…buy a gift for a child	…ein Geschenk für ein Kind kaufen *ine geshenk fewr ine kint kow-fen*
Can you recommend something?	Können Sie mir etwas empfehlen? *kur-nen zee mir et-vus em-pfay-len*
Do you have a box for it?	Haben Sie einen passenden Karton? *hah-ben zee ine-nen pah-senden kar-tohn*
Can you gift-wrap it?	Können Sie es als Geschenk verpacken? *kurn-nen zee es als geshenk fair-puk-ken*

die Halskette
dee Huls-ket-te
necklace

das Armband
dus arm-bunt
bracelet

die Uhr
dee oor
watch

die Manschettenknöpfe
dee mun-shetten-knurpfe
cufflinks

die Puppe
dee poo-pe
doll

das Kuscheltier
dus koo-shel-teer
soft toy

die Geldtasche
dee gelt-tush-e
wallet

die Pralinen
dee prah-lee-nen
chocolates

Have you anything cheaper?	Haben Sie etwas Billigeres? *hah-ben zee et-vus billy-gair-es*
Is there a reduction for cash?	Gibt es eine Ermäßigung bei Bargeldzahlung? *geept es ine-e air-mehsee-goong by bar-gelt-tsah-loong*
Is there a guarantee?	Gibt es eine Garantie? *geept es ine-e gah-run-tee*

You may hear...

- **Ist es ein Geschenk?**
  ist es ine geshenk
  Is it a present?

- **Soll ich es als Geschenk verpacken?**
  sohl ikh es als geshenk fair-pukken
  Shall I gift-wrap it?

PHOTOGRAPHY

I'd like this film developed	Können Sie diesen Film entwickeln *kurn-en zee dee-zen film ent-vee-keln*
When will it be ready?	Wann ist er fertig? *vun ist air fair-tik*
Do you have an express service?	Haben Sie einen Express-Service? *hah-ben zee ine-nen express-service*
Does it cost more?	Kostet das mehr? *kos-tet dus mair*
I'd like the one-hour service	Ich möchte gern den Einstunden-Service *ikh murkh-te gairn dain ine-shtoon-den-service*

die Digitalkamera
dee dee-ghee-tul-kah-meh-ra
digital camera

die Memory Card
dee memory card
memory card

die Filmrolle
dee film-rol-le
roll of film

das Fotoalbum
dus fo-to-ul-boom
photo album

der Bilderrahmen
dair bil-dair-rah-men
photo frame

Do you print digital photos?	Drucken Sie Digitalfotos? *droo-ken zee dee-ghee-tul-fo-tos*
Can you print from this memory stick?	Können Sie von diesem Memory Stick drucken? *kur-nen zee fon dee-zem memory stick droo-ken*

das Blitzlicht
dus blits-likht
flash gun

die Kamera
dee kah-meh-ra
camera

das Objektiv
dus ob-yek-teef
lens

die Kameratasche
dee kah-meh-ra-tush-e
camera bag

You may hear...

- **Welche Bildgröße möchten Sie?**
  vel-khe bilt-grur-se murkh-ten zee
  What size prints do you want?

- **Matt oder glänzend?**
  mutt oh-der glen-tsent
  Matt or gloss?

AT THE POST OFFICE

I'd like...	Ich möchte gern... *ikh murkh-te gairn*
...to register this letter	...diesen Brief per Einschreiben senden *dee-zen breef pair ine-shry-ben zen-den*
...to send this airmail	...diesen Brief per Luftpost senden *dee-zen breef pair looft-posst zen-den*
...three stamps, please	...drei Briefmarken, bitte *dry breef-marken bit-te*

der Briefumschlag
dair breef-oom-shlahk
envelope

die Briefmarken
dee breef-marken
stamps

die Ansichtskarte
dee un-zikhts-kar-te
postcard

die Luftpost
dee looft-posst
airmail

You may hear...

- **Was ist der Inhalt?**
  vus ist dair in-hult
  What are the contents?

- **Welchen Wert hat er?**
  vel-khen vairt hut air
  What is their value?

How much is…?	Was kostet… *vus kos-tet*
…a letter to…	…ein Brief nach… ? *ine breef nakh*
…a postcard to…	…eine Ansichtskarte nach… ? *ine-e un-zikhts-karte nakh*
…Great Britain	…Großbritannien *gros-bree-tun-nee-yen*

das Paket
dus pa-kayt
parcel

der Kurier
dair koo-reer
courier

der Briefkasten
dair breef-kuss-ten
postbox

der Briefträger
dair breef-tray-ger
postman

…the United States	…den Vereinigten Staaten *dain fair-eye-nik-ten shtah-ten*
…Canada	…Kanada *kah-nah-dah*
…Australia	…Australien *ows-trah-lee-en*
Can I have a receipt?	Kann ich eine Quittung haben? *kunn ikh ine-e kvit-toong hah-ben*

TELEPHONES

Where is the nearest phone box?

Wo ist die nächste
Telefonzelle?
*vo ist dee nekh-ste
tay-lay-fohn-tsel-le*

das Telefon
dus tay-lay-fohn
phone

das Handy
dus han-dee
mobile phone

die Telefonkarte
dee tay-lay-fohn-kar-te
phone card

die Telefonzelle
dee tay-lay-fohn-tsel-le
telephone box

das Münztelefon
dus mewnts-tay-lay-fohn
coin phone

der Anrufbeantworter
dair un-roof-bay-unt-vor-tair
answering machine

Who's speaking?	Mit wem spreche ich? *mit vaim shpre-khe ikh*
Hello, this is…	Hallo, hier spricht… *hul-lo heer shprikht*
I'd like to speak to…	Ich möchte gern mit… sprechen *ikh murkh-te gairn mit… shpre-khen*

INTERNET

Is there an internet café near here?	Gibt es ein Internetcafé in der Nähe? *geept es ine internet-café in dair nay-he*
How much do you charge?	Wie viel verlangen Sie? *vee feel fair-lun-gen zee*
Do you have wireless internet?	Haben Sie WLAN? *hah-ben zee veh-lun*
Can I check my emails?	Kann ich meine E-Mails checken? *kunn ikh my-ne e-mails tsheck-en*
I need to send an email	Ich muss eine E-Mail schicken *ikh moos ine-e e-mail shi-ken*
What's your email address?	Wie ist Ihre E-Mailadresse? *vee ist ee-re e-mail-ah-dres-se*
My email address is…	Meine E-Mailadresse ist… *my-ne e-mail-ah-dres-se ist*

der Laptop
dair lap-top
laptop

die Tastatur
dee tus-tah-toor
keyboard

die Website
dee web-site
website

die E-Mail
dee e-mail
email

SIGHTSEEING

Most towns have a tourist information office and
the staff will advise you on local places to visit as
well as city walks and bus tours. Opening hours
are usually 9.00am to 6.00pm Mondays to Fridays
and Saturday mornings. Many museums close
on Mondays as well as public holidays, so be sure
to check the opening times before visiting.

AT THE TOURIST OFFICE

Where is the tourist information office?	Wo ist das Fremdenverkehrsbüro? *vo ist dus frem-den-fer-kairs-bew-ro*
Can you...	Können Sie... *kur-nen zee*
...recommend a guided tour?	...eine Stadtführung empfehlen? *ine-e shtut-few-rung em-pfay-len*
...recommend an excursion?	...einen Ausflug empfehlen? *ine-nen ows-flook em-pfay-len*
Is there a museum or art gallery?	Gibt es hier ein Museum oder eine Kunstgalerie? *geept es heer ine moo-zay-oom ohder ine-e koonst-gal-le-ree*
Is it open to the public?	Ist es für die Öffentlichkeit zugänglich? *ist es fewr dee ur-fent-likh-kite tsoo-geng-likh*
Is there wheelchair access?	Gibt es Zugang für Rollstuhlfahrer? *geept es tsoo-gung fewr roll-shtool-fah-rer*
Does it...	Ist es... *ist es*
...close on Sundays?	...am Sonntag geschlossen? *um zon-tahk ge-shlos-sen*
...close on bank holidays?	...an Feiertagen geschlossen? *un fy-er-tah-gen ge-shlos-sen*
How long does it take to get there?	Wie lange dauert es bis dorthin? *vee lun-ge dow-ert es bis dort-hin*

VISITING PLACES

What time...	Um wie viel Uhr... *om vee-feel oor*
...do you open?	...öffnen Sie? *urf-nen zee*
...do you close?	...schließen Sie? *shlee-sen zee*
Two adults, please	Zwei Erwachsene, bitte *tsvy air-vakh-ze-ne bit-te*
A family ticket, please	Eine Familienkarte, bitte *ine-e fah-mee-lee-yen-kar-te bit-te*
How much does it cost?	Was kostet das? *vus kos-tet dus*
Are there reductions for...	Gibt es eine Ermäßigung für... *geept es ine-e er-mess-see-goong fewr*
...children?	...Kinder? *kin-der*
...students?	...Studenten? *shtoo-den-ten*

der Stadtplan
dair shtut-plun
street map

die Eintrittskarte
dee ine-trits-kar-te
entrance ticket

der Zugang für Rollstuhlfahrer
dair tsoo-gung fewr roll-shtool-fah-rer
wheelchair access

Can I buy a guidebook?	Kann ich einen Führer kaufen? *kunn ikh ine-nen few-rer kow-fen*
Is there…	Gibt es… *geept es*
…an audio-guide?	…einen Audioguide? *ine-nen owdeeyo-guide*
…a guided tour?	…eine Führung? *ine-ne few-roong*
…a lift?	…einen Lift? *ine-nen lift*
…a café?	…ein Café? *ine kuf-fay*
…a bus tour?	…eine Busrundfahrt? *ine-ne boos-roont-fart*
When is the next tour?	Wann ist die nächste Führung? *vun ist dee nekh-ste few-roong*

der Tourenbus
dair too-ren-boos
tour bus

You may hear…

- Haben Sie einen Studentenausweis?
hah-ben zee ine-nen shtoo-den-ten-ows-vice
Do you have a student card?

FINDING YOUR WAY

Excuse me	Entschuldigen Sie, bitte *ent-shool-dee-gen zee bit-te*
Can you help me?	Können sie mir helfen? *kur-nen zee mir hel-fen*
Is this the way to the museum?	Ist das der Weg zum Museum? *ist dus dair vayk tsoom moo-zay-oom*
How do I get to...?	Wie komme ich... ? *vee kom-me ikh*
...the town centre?	...zum Stadtzentrum? *tsoom shtut-tsen-troom*
...the station?	...zum Bahnhof? *tsoom bahn-hohf*
...the museum?	...zum Museum? *tsoom moo-zay-oom*
...the art gallery?	...zur Kunstgalerie? *tsoor koonst-gal-le-ree*
How long does it take?	Wie lange dauert das? *vee lun-ge dow-ert dus*
Is it far?	Ist es weit? *ist es vyte*
Can you show me on the map?	Können Sie es mir auf der Karte zeigen? *kur-nen zee es mir owf dair kar-te tsy-gen*

You may hear...

- **Es ist nicht weit.**
  es ist nikht vyte
  It's not far away.

- **Es ist 10 Minuten zu Fuß.**
  es ist tsayn mi-noo-ten tsoo foos
  It takes 10 minutes.

You may hear...

• **Wir sind hier** *veer zint heer*	We are here
• **Gehen Sie geradeaus...** *gay-en zee ge-rah-de-ows*	Keep straight on...
• **...bis ans Ende der Straße...** *bis uns en-de dair shtrah-se*	to the end of the street
• **...bis zur Ampel** *bis tsoor um-pel*	...to the traffic lights
• **...bis zum Hauptplatz** *bis tsoom howpt-pluts*	...to the main square
• **In diese Richtung** *in dee-ze rikh-toong*	This way
• **In die andere Richtung** *in dee un-dair-re rikh-toong*	That way
• **An der Ampel rechts abbiegen** *un dair um-pel rekhts up-bee-gen*	Turn right at the traffic lights
• **Am Museum links abbiegen** *um moo-zay-oom links up-bee-gen*	Turn left at the museum
• **Nehmen Sie die erste (Straße)** *nay-men zee dee airs-te (shtrah-se)*	Take the first street
• **links/rechts** *links/rekhts*	on the left/right
• **Sie stehen direkt davor** *zee shtay-en dee-rekht da-for*	It's in front of you
• **Es ist hinter Ihnen** *es ist hin-ter eenen*	It's behind you
• **Es ist Ihnen gegenüber** *es ist eenen gay-gen-ewber*	It's opposite you
• **Es ist neben...** *es ist nay-ben*	It's next to....
• **Es ist ausgeschildert** *es ist ows-ge-shildert*	It's signposted
• **Es ist dort drüben** *es ist dort drew-ben*	It's over there

PLACES TO VISIT

das Rathaus
dus raht-hows
town hall

die Brücke
dee brew-ke
bridge

das Museum
dus moo-zay-oom
museum

die Kunstgalerie
dee koonst-gal-le-ree
art gallery

das Denkmal
dus denk-mahl
monument

die Kirche
dee kir-khe
church

der Dom
dair dohm
cathedral

das Dorf
dus dorf
village

der Park
dair park
park

der Hafen
dair ha-fen
harbour

der Leuchtturm
dair loykht-toorm
lighthouse

der Weinberg
dair vine-bairk
vineyard

das Schloss
dus shloss
castle

die Küste
dee kew-ste
coast

der Wasserfall
dair vus-ser-fahl
waterfall

die Berge
dee bair-ge
mountains

OUTDOOR ACTIVITIES

Where can we...	Wo können wir... *vo kur-nen veer*
...go horse riding?	...reiten? *ry-ten*
...go fishing?	...angeln? *un-geln*
...go swimming?	...schwimmen? *shvim-men*
...go walking?	...wandern? *vun-dern*
Can we...	Können wir... *kur-nen veer*
...hire equipment?	...eine Ausrüstung mieten? *ine-e ows-rewst-toong mee-ten*
...have lessons?	...Unterricht nehmen? *oon-ter-rikht nay-men*
How much per hour?	Was kostet das pro Stunde? *vus kostet dus pro shtoonde*
I'm a beginner	Ich bin Anfänger/Anfängerin *ikh bin unfenger/unfengerin*
I'm quite experienced	Ich bin schon recht erfahren *ikh bin shon rekht air-fah-ren*
Where's the amusement park?	Wo ist der Vergnügungspark? *vo ist dair fair-gnew-goongs-park*
Can the children go on all the rides?	Sind Kinder auf allen Attraktionen erlaubt? *zint kin-der owf allen attrak-tsyoh-nen air-lowpt*
Is there a playground?	Gibt es einen Spielplatz? *geept es ine-nen shpeel-pluts*
Is it safe for children?	Ist er kindersicher? *ist air kin-der-zikher*

der Vergnügungspark
dair fair-gnew-goongs-park
fairground

der Erlebnispark
dair air-lep-nis-park
theme park

der Safaripark
dair safari-park
safari park

der Zoo
dair tsoh
zoo

der Spielplatz
dair shpeel-pluts
playground

das Picknick
dus pick-nick
picnic

das Angeln
dus an-geln
fishing

das Reiten
dus ry-ten
horse riding

SPORTS AND LEISURE

Germany and Austria can both offer the traveller a wide range of cultural events, entertainments and leisure activities. They have a strong musical tradition with superb opera houses and concert halls as well as renowned musical festivals. There is also a wide range of sports facilities on offer, from Alpine winter sports and climbing to hiking and cycling in the Black Forest and watersports on the many inland lakes and on the northern Baltic and North Sea coasts of Germany.

LEISURE TIME

I like...	Ich mag... *ikh mahk*
...art and painting	...Kunst und Malerei *koonst oont mah-ler-rye*
...films and cinema	...Filme und Kino *fil-me oont kee-no*
...the theatre	...das Theater *dus tay-ah-ter*
...opera	...die Oper *dee oh-per*
I prefer...	Ich mag lieber... *ikh mahk lee-ber*
...reading books	...lesen *lay-zen*
...listening to music	...Musik hören *moo-zeek hur-ren*
...watching sport	...Sport sehen *shport zay-en*
...playing games	...mitspielen *mit-shpee-len*
...going to concerts	...ins Konzert gehen *ins kon-tsehrt gay-en*
...dancing	...tanzen gehen *tun-tsen gay-en*
...going clubbing	...in die Disco gehen *in dee disco gay-en*
...going out with friends	...mit Freunden ausgehen *mit froyn-den ows-gay-en*
I don't like...	Ich mag nicht... *ikh mahk nikht*
That bores me	Das finde ich langweilig *dus fin-de ikh lung-vy-lik*
That doesn't interest me	Das interessiert mich nicht *dus in-ter-es-seert mikh nikht*

AT THE BEACH

Can I...	Kann ich... *kunn ikh*
...hire a jet ski?	...einen Jetski mieten? *ine-nen jetskee mee-ten*
...hire a beach umbrella?	...einen Sonnenschirm mieten? *ine-nen zon-nen-sheerm mee-ten*
...hire a surfboard?	...ein Surfboard leihen? *ine zurf-board ly-en*

das Strandlaken
dus shtrunt-lah-ken
beach towel

der Wasserball
dair vus-ser-bahl
beach ball

der Liegestuhl
dair lee-ge-shtool
deck chair

die Sonnenliege
dee zon-nen-lee-ge
sun lounger

You may hear...

• **Schwimmen verboten.**
shvim-men fair-bo-ten
No swimming

• **Der Strand ist gesperrt.**
dair shtrant ist ge-shpairt
Beach closed

• **Starke Strömung.**
shtar-ke shtrur-moong
Strong currents

die Sonnenbrille
dee zon-nen-bril-le
sunglasses

der Sonnenhut
dair zon-nen-hoot
sunhat

der Bikini
dair bee-kee-nee
bikini

das Sonnenschutzmittel
dus zon-nen-shoots-mittel
suntan lotion

die Schwimmflossen
dee shvim-flos-sen
flippers

die Maske/der Schnorchel
dee mas-ke/dair shnor-khel
mask/snorkel

How much does it cost?	Was kostet das? *vus kos-tet dus*
Can I go water-skiing?	Kann ich wasserskifahren? *kunn ikh vus-ser-shee-fah-ren*
Is there a lifeguard?	Ist ein Rettungsschwimmer da? *ist ine ret-toongs-shvim-mer dah*
Is it safe to…	Kann man… *kunn mun*
…swim here?	…hier schwimmen? *heer shvim-men*
…surf here?	…hier surfen? *heer zur-fen*

AT THE SWIMMING POOL

What time...	Um wie viel Uhr... *oom vee-feel oor*
...does the pool open?	...öffnet das Schwimmbad? *urf-net dus shvim-baht*
...does the pool close?	...schließt das Schwimmbad? *shleest dus shvim-baht*
Is it...	Ist es... *ist es*
...an indoor pool?	...ein Hallenbad? *ine hull-en-baht*
...an outdoor pool?	...ein Freibad? *ine fry-baht*
Is there a children's pool?	Gibt es ein Kinderbecken? *geept es ine kin-der-bek-ken*
Where are the changing rooms?	Wo sind die Umkleidekabinen? *vo zint dee oom-kly-de-kah-beenen*

die Schwimmflügel
dee shvim-flew-gel
armband

das Schwimmkissen
dus shvim-kis-sen
float

die Schwimmbrille
dee shvim-brill-le
swimming goggles

der Badeanzug
dair bah-de-un-tsook
swimsuit

AT THE GYM

die Rudermaschine
dee roo-der-mah-shee-ne
rowing machine

der Ellipsentrainer
dair el-lip-zen-trai-ner
cross trainer

der Stepper
dair step-per
step machine

das Trainingsrad
dus trai-nings-raht
exercise bike

Is there a gym?	Gibt es hier ein Fitnessstudio? *geept es heer ine fit-ness-shtoo-dee-yoh*
Is it free for guests?	Ist es für Gäste kostenlos? *ist es fewr ges-te kos-ten-los*
Do I have to wear trainers?	Muss ich Turnschuhe tragen? *moos ikh toorn-shoo-e trah-gen*
Do I need an induction session?	Muss ich an einer Einführung teilnehmen? *moos ikh un ine-er ine-few-roong tile-nay-men*
Do you hold...	Haben Sie... *hah-ben zee*
...aerobics classes?	...Aerobic-Kurse? *aerobic-koor-ze*
...Pilates classes?	...Pilates-Kurse? *pee-la-tes-koor-ze*
...yoga classes?	...Joga-Kurse? *yoga-koor-ze*

BOATING AND SAILING

Can I...	Kann ich... *kunn ikh*
...hire a dinghy?	...ein Dinghi mieten? *ine dinghy mee-ten*
...hire a windsurfer?	...einen Windsurfer mieten? *ine-nen vint-zur-fer mee-ten*
...a canoe?	...ein Kanu mieten? *ine kah-noo mee-ten*

die Schwimmweste
dee shvim-ves-te
life jacket

der Kompass
dair kom-pus
compass

...hire a rowing boat?	...ein Ruderboot mieten? *ine roo-der-boht mee-ten*
Do you offer sailing lessons?	Geben Sie Segelunterricht? *gay-ben zee zay-gel-oon-ter-rikht*
Do you have a mooring?	Haben Sie einen Liegeplatz? *hah-ben zee ine-nen lee-ge-pluts*
How much is it for the night?	Wie viel kostet es pro Nacht? *vee-feel kos-tet es pro nakht*
Where can I buy gas?	Wo kann ich Gas kaufen? *vo kunn ikh gus kow-fen*
Where is the marina?	Wo ist der Jachthafen? *vo ist dair yakht-hah-fen*
Are there life jackets?	Sind Schwimmwesten vorhanden? *zint shvim-ves-ten for-han-den*

WINTER SPORTS

I would like to...	Ich möchte gern... *ikh murkh-te gairn*
...hire some skis	...Skier leihen *shee-er ly-hen*
...hire some ski boots	...Skistiefel leihen *shee-shtee-fel ly-hen*
...hire some poles	...Skistöcke leihen *shee-shtur-ke ly-hen*
...hire a snowboard	...ein Snowboard leihen *ine snow-board ly-hen*
...hire a helmet	...einen Sturzhelm leihen *ine-nen shtoorts-helm ly-hen*
When does...	Wann... *vun*
...the chair lift start?	...fährt der erste Sessellift? *fairt dair airs-te zes-sel-lift*
...the cable car finish?	...fährt die letzte Seilbahn? *fairt dee lets-te zile-bahn*
How much is a lift pass?	Was kostet ein Liftpass? *vus kos-tet ine lift-pass*
Can I take skiing lessons?	Kann ich Skiunterricht nehmen? *kunn ikh shee-oon-ter-rikht nay-men*
Where are the nursery slopes?	Wo sind die Idiotenhügel? *vo zint dee ee-dee-yoten-hew-gel*

You may hear...

- **Sind Sie Anfänger/ Anfängerin?**
  zind zee un-fenger/ un-fenger-in
  Are you a beginner?

- **Ich brauche eine Kaution.**
  ikh brow-khe ine-e kow-tsee-yon
  I need a deposit.

BALL GAMES

I like playing…	Ich spiele gern… *ikh shpee-le gairn*
…football	…Fußball *foos-bahl*
…tennis	…Tennis *tennis*
…golf	…Golf *golf*
…badminton	…Badminton *badminton*
…squash	…Squash *skwosh*
…baseball	…Baseball *baseball*
Where is the nearest…	Wo ist der nächste… *vo ist dair nekh-ste*
…tennis court?	…Tennisplatz? *tennis-pluts*
…golf course?	…Golfplatz? *golf-pluts*

der Fußball
dair foos-bahl
football

die Wristbänder
dee rist-ben-der
wristbands

der Korb
dair korp
basket

der Baseballhandschuh
dair base-ball-hunt-shoo
baseball mitt

Can I…	Kann ich… *kunn ikh*
…book a court for two hours?	…einen Platz für zwei Stunden buchen? *ine-nen pluts fewr tsvy shtoon-den boo-khen*
…book a court at three o'clock?	…einen Platz für drei Uhr buchen? *ine-nen pluts fewr dry oor boo-khen*
What shoes are allowed?	Welche Schuhe sind erlaubt? *vel-khe shoo-he zint air-lowpt*
Can I…	Kann ich… *kunn ikh*
…hire a tennis racquet?	…einen Tennisschläger mieten? *ine-nen tennis-shlay-ger mee-ten*
…hire some balls?	…einige Bälle mieten? *ine-ige bell-le mee-ten*
…hire a set of clubs?	…ein Golfset mieten? *ine golf-set mee-ten*

der Tennisschläger
dair tennis-shlay-ger
tennis racquet

die Tennisbälle
dee tennis-bell-le
tennis balls

der Golfball und das Golf-Tee
dair golf-bahl oont dus golf-tee
golf ball and tee

der Golfschläger
dair golf-shlay-ger
golf club

GOING OUT

Where is...	Wo ist... *vo ist*
...the opera house?	...die Oper? *dee oh-pair*
...a jazz club?	...ein Jazzclub? *ine jazz-kloob*
Do I have to book in advance?	Muss ich vorab buchen? *moos ikh for-up boo-khen*
I'd like...tickets	Ich möchte...Karten *ikh murkh-te...kar-ten*
I'd like seats...	Ich möchte Sitze... *ikh murkh-te zit-se*
...at the back	...hinten *hin-ten*
...at the front	...vorne *for-ne*
...in the middle	...in der Mitte *in dair mi-te*
...in the gallery	...auf dem Rang *owf daim rung*
Can I buy a programme?	Kann ich ein Programm kaufen? *kunn ikh ine pro-gramm kow-fen*
Is there live music?	Wird live gespielt? *veert live ge-shpeelt*

You may hear...

- **Schalten Sie Ihr Handy aus.**
  shulten zee eer handy ows
  Turn off your mobile.

- **Kehren Sie zu Ihren Plätzen zurück.**
  kair-ren zee tsoo ee-ren plet-sen tsoo-rewk
  Return to your seats.

das Theater
dus tay-ah-ter
theatre

das Openhaus
dus oh-pairn-hows
opera house

der Musiker
dair moo-zee-ker
musician

der Pianist
dair pee-ah-nist
pianist

der Sänger/die Sängerin
dair zen-ger/dee zen-gerin
singer

das Ballett
dus bah-let
ballet

das Kino
dus kee-no
cinema

das Popkorn
dus pop-corn
popcorn

das Kasino
dus kah-zee-no
casino

der Nachtclub
dair nakht-kloob
nightclub

GALLERIES AND MUSEUMS

What are the opening hours?	Was sind die Öffnungszeiten? *vus zint dee urf-noongs-tsy-ten*
Are there guided tours in English?	Gibt es englische Führungen? *geept es eng-lishe few-run-gen*
When does the tour leave?	Wann beginnt die Besichtigungstour? *vun beginnt dee be-zikh-tee-goongs-toor*
How much does it cost?	Wie viel kostet es? *vee-feel kos-tet es*
How long does it take?	Wie lange dauert es? *vee lun-ghe dowert es*
Do you have an audio guide?	Haben Sie einen Audioguide? *hah-ben zee ine-nen ow-dee-oh-guide*
Do you have a guidebook in English?	Haben Sie einen englischen Führer? *hah-ben zee ine-nen eng-lishen few-rer*
Is (flash) photography allowed?	Ist das Fotografieren (mit Blitzlicht) erlaubt? *ist dus fo-to-gra-fee-ren (mit blits-likht) air-lowpt*

die Statue
dee shta-too-e
statue

die Büste
dee bews-te
bust

Can you direct me to…?	Wie finde ich…? *vee fin-de ikh*
I'd really like to see the pictures	Ich möchte gern die Bilder sehen *ikh murkh-te gairn dee bil-der zay-en*
Who painted this?	Wer hat das gemalt? *vair hut dus ge-mahlt*
How old is it?	Wie alt ist es? *vee ult ist es*

das Gemälde
dus ge-mel-de
painting

der Stich
dair shtikh
engraving

die Zeichnung
dee tsykh-noong
drawing

das Manuskript
dus mah-noos-kript
manuscript

Are there wheelchair ramps?	Gibt es Rollstuhlrampen? *geept es roll-shtool-rum-pen*
Is there a lift?	Ist ein Lift da? *ist ine lift dah*
Where are the toilets?	Wo sind die Toiletten? *vo zint dee twah-let-ten*
I've lost my group	Ich habe meine Gruppe verloren *ikh hah-be my-ne groo-pe fair-lo-ren*

HOME ENTERTAINMENT

How do I...	Wie...? *vee*
...turn the television on?	...stelle ich den Fernseher an? *shtelle ikh dain fairnzayer un*
...change channels?	...wechsle ich die Kanäle? *vekhs-le ikh dee kahnayle*
...turn the volume up?	...stelle ich den Ton lauter? *shtel-le ikh dain tohn lowtair*
...turn the volume down?	...mache ich den Ton leiser? *ma-khe ikh den tohn lyzair*
Do you have satellite TV?	Haben Sie Satelliten-Fernsehen? *hah-ben zee za-tel-lee-ten-fairnzayen*
Where can I...	Wo kann ich... *vo kunn ikh*
...buy a DVD?	...eine DVD kaufen? *ine-e deh fow deh kow-fen*
...buy a music CD?	...eine Musik-CD kaufen? *ine-e moozik-tseh-deh kow-fen*

der Breitbild-Fernseher
dair brite-bilt-fairnzayer
widescreen TV

der DVD-Player
dair deh fow deh player
DVD player

die Fernbedienung
dee fairn-be-dee-nung
remote control

das Videospiel
dus vee-de-oh-shpeel
video game

der CD-Spieler
dair tseh-deh-shpee-ler
CD player

der iPod
dair iPod
iPod

das Radio
dus rah-dee-oh
radio

der Laptop
dair lap-top
laptop

die Maus
dee mows
mouse

Can I use this to…	Kann ich damit… *kunn ikh dah-mit*
…go online?	…Online gehen? *on-line gay-en*
Is it broadband/wifi?	Ist es ein Breitband-/ WLAN-Anschluss? *ist es ine brite-bant/ veh-lun-un-shloos*
How do…	Wie… *Vee*
…I log on?	…logge ich mich ein? *log-ge ikh mikh ine*
…I log out?	…logge ich mich aus? *log-ge ikh mikh ows*

HEALTH

If you are an EU national, you are entitled to free emergency medical treatment in both Germany and Austria, but you will have to produce your European Health Insurance Card. It is always a good idea to familiarize yourself with a few basic phrases for use in an emergency or in case you need to visit a pharmacy or doctor.

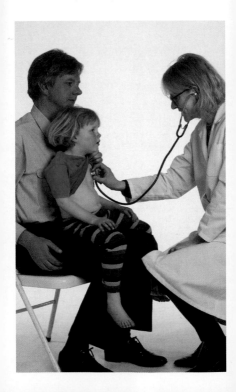

USEFUL PHRASES

I need a doctor	Ich brauche einen Arzt *ikh brow-khe ine-nen artst*
I would like...	Kann ich... *kunn ikh*
...an appointment today	...heute einen Termin haben *hoy-te ine-nen tair-min hah-ben*
...an appointment tomorrow	...morgen einen Termin haben *mor-gen ine-nen tair-min hah-ben*
It's very urgent	Es ist sehr dringend *es ist zair drin-gent*
I have a European Health Insurance Card	Ich habe eine Europäische Krankenversicherungskarte *ikh hah-be ine-e oyro-pay-ee-shuh krunk-en-fair-zikher-oongs-kar-te*
I have health insurance	Ich habe eine Krankenversicherung *ikh hah-be ine-e krunk-en-fair-zikher-oong*
Can I have a receipt?	Kann ich eine Quittung haben? *kunn ikh ine-ne kvit-toong hah-ben*
Where is...	Wo ist... *vo ist*
...the nearest pharmacy?	...die nächste Apotheke? *dee nekh-ste apo-tay-ke*
...the nearest doctor's surgery?	...die nächste Arztpraxis? *dee nekh-ste artst-pra-xis*
...the nearest hospital?	...das nächste Krankenhaus? *dus nekh-ste krunken-hows*
...the nearest dentist?	...der nächste Zahnarzt? *dair nekh-ste tsahn-artst*

AT THE PHARMACY

What can I take for...?	Was hilft gegen...? *vus hilft gay-gen*
How many should I take?	Wie viele soll ich davon nehmen? *vee-feel-e zoll ikh dah-fon nay-men*
Is it safe for children?	Ist es für Kinder ungefährlich? *ist es fewr kin-der oon-ge-fair-likh*
Are there side effects?	Gibt es Nebenwirkungen? *geept es nayben-veer-koon-gen*
Do you have that...	Haben Sie das... *hah-ben zee dus*
...as tablets?	...als Tabletten? *uls tub-let-ten*
...as a spray	...als Spray? *uls spray*
...in capsule form?	...in Kapselform? *in kup-sel-form*
I'm allergic to...	Ich bin allergisch gegen... *ikh bin ul-lair-gish gay-gen*
I'm already taking...	Ich nehme bereits... *ikh nay-me be-rites*
Do I need a prescription?	Brauche ich ein Rezept? *brow-khe ikh ine ray-tsept*

You may hear...

- **Sie nehmen das...mal am Tag.**
 zee nay-men dus...mul um tahk
 Take this...times a day.

- **Vor den Mahlzeiten.**
 for dain mahl-tsyten
 Before eating.

- **Während der Mahlzeiten.**
 vairent dair mahl-tsyten
 With food.

die Bandage
dee bun-dah-she
bandage

das Pflaster
dus pflus-ter
plaster

die Kapsel
dee kup-sel
capsule

die Tablette
dee tub-let-te
pill

der Inhalator
dair in-ha-la-tor
inhaler

das Zäpfchen
dus tsepf-khen
suppository

die Tropfen
dee tropf-en
drops

das Spray
dus shpray
spray

die Salbe
dee zul-be
ointment

der Sirup
dair zee-roop
syrup

THE HUMAN BODY

I have hurt my knee

Ich habe mir das Knie verletzt
ikh hah-be meer dus k-nee fair-letst

der Ellbogen
dair el-bo-gen
elbow

der Arm
dair arm
arm

der Kopf
dair kopf
head

die Schulter
dee shool-ter
shoulder

der Nacken
dair nak-ken
neck

die Brust
dee broost
chest

der Bauch
dair bowkh
stomach

das Bein
dus bine
leg

das Knie
dus k-nee
knee

der Fuß
dair foos
foot

FACE

die Haut
dee howt
skin

das Ohr
dus ohr
ear

das Muttermal
dus mooter-mal
mole

das Kinn
dus kin
chin

das Auge
dus ow-ge
eye

die Wange
dee vun-ge
cheek

der Kiefer
dair kee-fer
jaw

der Mund
dair moont
mouth

die Nase
dee nah-ze
nose

HAND

FOOT

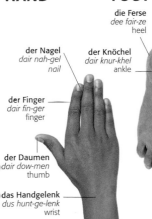

der Nagel
dair nah-gel
nail

der Finger
dair fin-ger
finger

der Daumen
dair dow-men
thumb

das Handgelenk
dus hunt-ge-lenk
wrist

die Ferse
dee fair-ze
heel

der Knöchel
dair knur-khel
ankle

die Zehe
dee tsay-he
toe

FEELING ILL

I don't feel well	Ich fühle mich nicht wohl *ikh few-le mikh nikht vohl*
I feel ill	Ich bin krank *ikh bin krunk*
I have...	Ich habe... *ikh hah-be*
...an ear ache	...Ohrenschmerzen *oh-ren-shmairt-sen*
...a stomach ache	...Bauchschmerzen *bowkh-shmairt-sen*
...a sore throat	...Halsschmerzen *huls-shmairt-sen*
...a temperature	...Fieber *fee-ber*
...hayfever	...Heuschnupfen *hoy-shnoop-fen*
...constipation	...Verstopfung *fair-shtopf-oong*
...diarrhoea	...Durchfall *doorkh-full*
...toothache	...Zahnschmerzen *tsahn-shmairt-sen*
I've been...	Mich hat... *mikh hut*
...stung by a bee/wasp	...eine Biene/Wespe gestochen *ine-e bee-ne/ves-pe ge-shto-khen*
...stung by a jellyfish	...eine Qualle gestochen *ine-e kval-le ge-shto-khen*
I've been...	Mich hat... *mikh hut*
...bitten by a snake	...eine Schlange gebissen *ine-e shlun-ge ge-bis-sen*
...bitten by a dog	...ein Hund gebissen *ine hoont ge-bis-sen*

INJURIES

die Schnittwunde
dee shnit-voon-de
cut

die Schramme
dee shrum-me
graze

die Prellung
dee prel-loong
bruise

der Splitter
dair shplit-ter
splinter

der Sonnenbrand
dair zon-nen-brunt
sunburn

die Brandwunde
dee brunt-voon-de
burn

die Bisswunde
dee bis-voon-de
bite

die Stichwunde
dee shtikh-voon-de
sting

die Verstauchung
dee fair-shtow-khung
sprain

der Bruch
dair brookh
fracture

AT THE DOCTOR

I'm...	Ich... *ikh*
...vomiting	...muss mich erbrechen *moos mikh air-brekhen*
...bleeding	...blute *bloo-te*
I'm feeling dizzy	Mir ist schwindlig *meer ist shvind-lik*
I'm feeling faint	Ich fühle mich matt *ikh few-le mikh mut*
I'm pregnant	Ich bin schwanger *ikh bin shvun-ger*
I'm diabetic	Ich bin Diabetiker/ Diabetikerin *ikh bin dee-ar-bay-ti-kair/ dee-ar-bay-ti-kair-in*
I'm epileptic	Ich bin Epileptikerin/ Epileptiker *ikh bin eh-pee-lep-ti-kair/ eh-pee-lep-ti-kair-in*
I have arthritis	Ich habe Arthritis *ikh hah-be ar-tree-tis*
I have heart condition	Ich bin herzkrank *ikh bin hairts-krunk*
I have high blood pressure	Ich habe hohen Blutdruck *ikh hah-be ho-hen bloot-drook*

You may hear...

- **Was fehlt Ihnen?**
  vus failt ee-nen
  What's wrong?

- **Wo tut es weh?**
  vo toot es vay
  Where does it hurt?

ILLNESS

die Kopfschmerzen
dee kopf-shmairt-sen
headache

das Nasenbluten
dus nah-zen-bloo-ten
nosebleed

der Husten
dair hoos-ten
cough

das Nießen
dus nee-sen
sneeze

die Erkältung
dee air-kel-tung
cold

die Grippe
dee grip-pe
flu

das Asthma
dus asth-mah
asthma

der Krampf
dair krumpf
cramps

die Übelkeit
dee ew-bel-kite
nausea

der Ausschlag
dair ows-shlahk
rash

AT THE HOSPITAL

Can you help me?	Können Sie mir helfen? *kurn-nen zee mir hel-fen*
I need…	Ich brauche… *ikh brow-ke*
…a doctor	…einen Arzt *ine-nen artst*
…a nurse	…eine Krankenschwester *ine-e krun-ken-shves-ter*
Where is…	Wo ist… *vo ist*
…the accident and emergency department?	…die Unfallstation? *dee oon-full-shta-tsee-yon*
…the children's ward?	…die Kinderstation *dee kin-der-shtah-tsee-yon*
…the X-ray department?	…die Röntgenabteilung *dee rurnt-gen-up-ty-loong*
…the waiting room?	…das Wartezimmer *dus var-te-tsim-mer*

die Injektion
dee in-yek-tsee-yon
injection

die Blutprobe
dee bloot-proh-be
blood test

das Röntgenbild
dus rurnt-gen-bilt
X-ray

der Ultraschall
dair ool-tra-shul
scan

…the intensive care unit?	…die Intensivstation *dee in-tenseev-shta-tsee-yon*
…the lift/stairs?	…der Lift/die Treppe? *dair Lift/dee trep-pe*
I think I've broken my arm	Ich glaube, ich habe mir den Arm gebrochen *ikh glow-be ikh hah-be mir dain arm ge-brokhen*
Do I need…	Brauche ich… *brow-khe ikh*
…an injection?	…eine Injektion? *ine-e in-yek-tsee-yon*
…antibiotics?	…Antibiotika? *anti-bee-oh-tee-kah*
…an operation?	…eine Operation? *ine-e o-pay-rah-tsee-yon*
Will it hurt?	Tut das weh? *toot dus vay*
How long will it take?	Wie lange wird es dauern? *vee lun-ge virt es dow-ern*

der Rollstuhl
dair roll-shtool
wheelchair

die Wiederbelebung
dee vee-der-be-lay-boong
resuscitation

die Schiene
dee shee-ne
splint

der Verband
dair fair-bunt
dressing

EMERGENCIES

In you are involved in an accident in Germany, you must dial 110 for the police (*Polizei*), whether or not there are injuries. Use the same number to call an ambulance (*Krankenwagen*), or 112 for the fire brigade (*Feurwehr*). If you are the victim of a crime or you lose your passport and money or other possessions, you should report the incident to the police without delay.

IN AN EMERGENCY

Help!	Hilfe! *hil-fe*
Please go away!	Gehen Sie bitte! *gay-en zee bit-te*
Let go!	Loslassen! *lohs-las-sen*
Stop! Thief!	Halt! Diebstahl! *hult deep-shtahl*
Call the police!	Rufen Sie die Polizei! *roo-fen zee dee po-lit-sye*
Get a doctor!	Holen Sie einen Arzt! *ho-len zee ine-nen artst*
I need...	Ich brauche... *ikh brow-khe*
...the police	...die Polizei *dee po-lit-sye*
...the fire brigade	...die Feuerwehr *dee foyer-vair*
...an ambulance	...einen Krankenwagen *ine-nen krun-ken-vah-gen*
It's very urgent	Es ist dringend *es ist drin-gent*
Where is...	Wo ist... *vo ist*
...the British embassy?	...die Britische Botschaft? *dee bri-tishe boht-shaft*
...the British consul?	...das Britische Konsulat? *dus bri-tishe kon-zoo-lut*
...the police station?	...die Polizeiwache? *dee po-lit-sye-vakhe*
...the hospital?	...das Krankenhaus? *dus krun-ken-hows*

ACCIDENTS

I need to make a telephone call	Ich muss telefonieren *ikh moos tay-lay-fo-nee-ren*
I'd like to report an accident	Ich möchte einen Unfall melden *ikh murkh-te ine-nen oon-fal mel-den*
I've crashed my car	Ich habe einen Autounfall gehabt *ikh hah-be ine-nen ow-toe oon-fall ge-hupt*
The registration number is...	Das amtliche Kennzeichen ist... *dus amt-likh-e ken-tsye-khen ist*
I'm at...	Ich befinde mich... *ikh be-fin-de mikh*
Please come quickly!	Kommen Sie bitte schnell! *kom-men zee bit-te shnel*
Someone's injured	Jemand ist verletzt *yay-munt ist fair-letst*
Someone's been knocked down	Jemand ist überfahren worden *yay-munt ist ew-ber-fah-ren vor-den*
There's a fire at my home	Bei mir ist ein Feuer ausgebrochen *by mir ist ine foy-er ows-ge-brokhen*

You may hear...

• **Welchen Notdienst brauchen Sie?**
vel-khen noht-deenst brow-khen zee
Which service do you require?

• **Was ist passiert?**
vus ist pah-seert
What happened?

EMERGENCY SERVICES

der Krankenwagen
dair krun-ken-vah-gen
ambulance

die Feuerwehrleute
dee foyer-vair-loy-te
firefighters

das Feuerwehrauto
dus foyer-vair-ow-toe
fire engine

der Feueralarm
dair foyer-ah-larm
fire alarm

der Hydrant
dair hew-drant
hydrant

der Feuerlöscher
dair foyer-lur-sher
fire extinguisher

die Handschellen
dee hunt-shel-len
handcuffs

das Polizeiauto
dus po-lit-sye-ow-toe
police car

der Polizist
dair po-lit-sist
policeman

POLICE AND CRIME

I want to report a crime	Ich möchte eine Anzeige machen *ikh murkh-te ine-e un-tsye-ge makhen*
I've been...	Ich bin... *ikh bin*
...robbed	...bestohlen worden *be-shtoh-len vor-den*
...mugged	...Opfer eines Straßenraubs geworden *op-fer ine-es shtra-sen-rowps ge-vor-den*
...raped	...vergewaltigt worden *fair-ge-vul-tigt vor-den*
I've been burgled	Bei mir ist eingebrochen worden *by mir ist ine-ge-brokhen vor-den*
Someone has...	Jemand hat... *yay-munt hut*
...stolen my car	...mein Auto gestohlen *mine ow-toe ge-shtoh-len*
...stolen my money	...mein Geld gestohlen *mine gelt ge-shtoh-len*
...stolen my traveller's cheques	...meine Reiseschecks gestohlen *my-ne rye-ze-shecks ge-shtoh-len*

You may hear...

- **Wann ist es passiert?**
  vun ist es pah-seert
  When did it happen?

- **Gibt es einen Zeugen?**
  geept es ine-nen tsoy-gen
  Was there a witness?

- **Wie sah er aus?**
  vee zah air ows
  What did he look like?

I'd like to…	Ich möchte… *ikh murkh-te*
…speak to a senior officer	…mit einem leitenden Beamten sprechen *mit ine-nem ly-ten-den bay-um-ten shpray-khen*
…speak to a policewoman	…mit einer Sicherheitsbeamtin sprechen *mit ine-er zikh-er-hites-be-um-tin shpray-khen*
I need…	Ich brauche… *ikh brow-khe*
…an interpreter	…einen Dolmetscher *ine-nen dol-met-sher*
…to make a phone call	Ich muss telefonieren *ikh moos tay-lay-fo-nee-ren*
I'm very sorry, officer	Das tut mir leid, Herr Kommissar *dus toot mir lite herr kom-mee-sar*
Here is…	Hier ist… *heer ist*
…my driving licence	…mein Führerschein *mine few-rer-shine*
…my insurance	…meine Versicherung *my-ne fair-zikh-eroong*

You may hear…

- Ihren Führerschein, bitte.
  ee-ren few-rer-shine bit-te
  Your licence, please.

- Ihre Zulassungsnummer?
  ee-re tsoo-las-sungs-noo-mer
  Your registation number?

AT THE GARAGE

Where is the nearest garage?	Wo ist die nächste Werkstatt? *vo ist dee nekh-ste vairk-stut*
Can you do repairs?	Machen Sie Reparaturen? *makh-en zee re-pah-ra-tooren*
I need...	Ich brauche... *ikh brow-khe*
...a new tyre	...einen neuen Reifen *ine-nen noy-en rye-fen*
...a new exhaust	...einen neuen Auspuff *ine-nen noy-en ows-poof*
...a new windscreen	...eine neue Windschutzscheibe *ine-e noy-e vint-shoots-shy-be*
...a new bulb	...eine neue Glühbirne *ine-e noy-e glew-beer-ne*
...new wiper blades	...neue Wischerblätter *noy-e visher-blet-ter*
Do you have one in stock?	Haben Sie Teile auf Lager? *hah-ben zee ty-le owf lah-ger*
Can you replace this?	Können Sie das austauschen? *kur-nen zee dus ows-tow-shen*
The...is not working	Der/die/das...funktioniert nicht *dair/dee/dus foonk-tsee-yoneert nikht*
Is it serious?	Ist es etwas Ernsthaftes? *ist es et-vus airnst-huf-tes*
How long will it take?	Wie lange wird es dauern? *vee lun-ge veert es dow-ern*
When will it be ready?	Wann wird es fertig sein? *vun veert es fer-tik zine*
How much will it cost?	Wie teuer wird es? *vee toy-er veert es*

CAR BREAKDOWN

My car has broken down	Mein Auto hat eine Panne *mine ow-toe hut ine-e pun-e*
Please can you help me?	Können Sie mir helfen? *kur-nen zee mir hel-fen*
Please come to…	Bitte kommen Sie zu… *bit-te kom-men zee tsoo*
I have a puncture	Ich habe einen Platten *ikh hah-be ine-nen plut-ten*
Can you help change the wheel?	Können Sie mir beim Reifenwechsel helfen? *kur-nen zee mir bym rye-fen-vek-sel hel-fen*
I need a new tyre	Ich brauche einen neuen Reifen *ikh brow-khe ine-nen noy-en rye-fen*
My car won't start	Mein Wagen springt nicht an *mine vah-gen shpringt nikht un*
The engine is overheating	Der Motor wird zu heiß *dair mo-tor veert tsoo hice*
Can you fix it?	Können Sie das reparieren? *kur-nen zee dus re-pah-reer-en*
I've run out of petrol	Mir ist das Benzin ausgegangen *mir ist dus ben-tseen ows-ge-gun-gen*

You may hear...

- **Brauchen Sie Hilfe?**
  brow-khen zee hil-fe
  Do you need any help?

- **Wo liegt denn das Problem?**
  vo leegt den dus prob-laym
  What is the problem?

LOST PROPERTY

I've…	Ich habe… *ikh hah-be*
…lost my money	…mein Geld verloren *mine gelt fair-lo-ren*
…lost my keys	…meine Schlüssel verloren *my-ne shlews-sel fair-lo-ren*
…lost my glasses	…meine Brille verloren *my-ne bril-le fair-lo-ren*
My luggage is missing	Mein Gepäck ist verloren gegangen *mine ge-pek ist fair-lo-ren ge-gun-gen*
Has it turned up yet?	Ist es schon aufgetaucht? *ist es shon owf-ge-towkht*

die Brieftasche
dee breef-tash-e
wallet

die Geldbörse
dee gelt-bur-se
purse

die Aktentasche
dee uk-ten-tush-e
briefcase

die Handtasche
dee hunt-tush-e
handbag

der Koffer
dair kof-fer
suitcase

der Reisescheck
dair rye-ze-shek
traveller's cheque

die Kreditkarte
dee kray-deet-kar-te
credit card

der Pass
dair pahs
passport

die Kamera
dee ka-me-ra
camera

das Handy
dus han-dee
mobile phone

I need to phone my insurance company	Ich muss meine Versicherung anrufen *ikh moos my-ne fair-zikh-air-oong un-roof-en*
Can I put a stop on my credit cards?	Kann ich meine Kreditkarten sperren? *kunn ikh my-ne kray-deet-kar-ten shpair-ren*
My name is...	Mein Name ist... *mine nah-me ist*
My policy number is...	Meine Versicherungsnummer ist... *my-ne fair-zikh-air-oongs-noo-mer ist*
My address is...	Meine Adresse ist... *my-ne ad-res-se ist*
My contact number is...	Meine Telefonnummer ist... *my-ne tay-lay-fohn-noo-mer ist*
My email address is...	Meine E-Mailadresse ist... *my-ne email-adres-se ist*

MENU GUIDE

This guide lists the most common terms you may encounter on German menus or when shopping for food. If you can't find an exact phrase, try looking up its component parts.

A

Aal eel
am Spieß on the spit
Ananas pineapple
Äpfel apples
Apfel im Schlafrock baked apple in puff pastry
Apfelsaft apple juice
Apfelsinen oranges
Apfelstrudel apple strudel
Apfeltasche apple turnover
Apfelwein cider
Aprikosen apricots
Arme Ritter bread soaked in milk and egg then fried
Artischocken artichokes
Auberginen aubergines
Auflauf sweet or savoury gratin dish
Aufschnitt cold meats
Austern oysters

B

Backobst dried fruit
Backpflaume prune
Baiser meringue
Balkansalat cabbage and pepper salad
Bananen bananas
Bandnudeln ribbon noodles
Basilikum basil
Bauernauflauf bacon and potato omelette
Bauernfrühstück fried potato, bacon, and egg
Bauernomelett bacon and potato omelette
Bechamelkartoffeln potatoes in a creamy sauce

Beckenoffe layered meat and potato casserole
Bedienung service
Beilagen side dishes
Berliner jam doughnut
Bier beer
Birnen pears
Biskuit sponge cake
Bismarckhering filleted pickled herring
Blätterteig puff pastry
blau cooked in vinegar; virtually raw (as in steak cooked "bleu")
Blumenkohl cauliflower
blutig rare (as in steak)
Blutwurst black pudding
Bockwurst large frankfurter sausage
Bohnen beans
Bouillon clear soup
Braten roast meat
Brathering pickled and fried herring, served cold
Bratkartoffeln fried potatoes
Bratwurst grilled pork sausage
Brot bread
Brötchen roll
Brühwurst large frankfurter
Brust breast
Bückling smoked red herring
Buletten burgers; rissoles
Bunte Platte mixed platter
Burgundersoße Burgundy wine sauce
Buttercremetorte cream cake
Buttermilch buttermilk

C

Champignons mushrooms
Cordon bleu veal cordon bleu
Currywurst mit Pommes curried pork sausage with chips

D

Dampfnudeln sweet yeast dumpling
Deutsches Beefsteak minced meat or patty
Dicke Bohnen broad beans
Dillsoße dill sauce
durchgebraten well-done
durchwachsen with fat
durchwachsener Speck streaky bacon

E

Eier eggs
Eierauflauf omelette
Eierkuchen pancake
Eierspeise scrambled eggs
eingelegt pickled
Eintopf stew
Eintopfgericht stew
Eis ice
Eisbecher sundae
Eisbein knuckle of pork
Eisschokolade iced chocolate
Eissplittertorte ice chip cake
Endiviensalat endive salad
englisch rare
Entenbraten roast duck
entgrätet boned (fish)
Erbsen peas
Erdbeertorte strawberry cake
Essig vinegar

F

Falscher Hase meat loaf
Fasan pheasant
Fenchel fennel
Fett fat
Filet fillet (steak)
Fisch fish

Fischfrikadellen fishcakes
Fischstäbchen fish fingers
Flädlesuppe consommé with pancake strips
flambiert flambéed
Fleischbrühe bouillon
Fleischkäse meat loaf
Fleischklößchen meatball(s)
Fleischpastete meat vol-au-vent
Fleischsalat diced meat salad with mayonnaise
Fleischwurst pork sausage
Fond meat juices
Forelle trout
Forelle Müllerin (Art) pan-fried trout with butter and lemon
Frikadelle rissole
Frikassee fricassee
fritiert (deep-) fried
Froschschenkel frog's legs
Fruchtsaft fruit juice
Frühlingsrolle spring roll

G

Gans goose
Gänseleberpastete goose-liver pâté
garniert garnished
Gebäck pastries, cakes
gebacken baked
gebraten roast
gedünstet steamed
Geflügel poultry
Geflügelleberragout chicken liver ragoût
gefüllt stuffed
gefüllte Kalbsbrust stuffed breast of veal
gekocht boiled
Gelee jelly
gemischter Salat mixed salad
Gemüse vegetable(s)
Gemüseplatte assorted vegetables
gepökelt salted, pickled
geräuchert smoked
Gericht dish

geschmort braised, stewed
Geschnetzeltes strips of fried meat in cream sauce
gespickt larded
Getränke beverages
Gewürze spices
Gewürzgurken gherkins
Goldbarsch type of perch
Götterspeise jelly
gratiniert au gratin
Grieß semolina
Grießklößchen semolina dumplings
grüne Bohnen French beans
grüne Nudeln green pasta
grüner Aal fresh eel
Grünkohl (curly) kale
Gulasch goulash
Gulaschsuppe goulash soup
Gurkensalat cucumber salad

H, I

Hackfleisch mince
Hähnchen chicken
Hähnchenkeule chicken leg
Haifischflossensuppe shark-fin soup
Hammelbraten roast mutton
Hammelfleisch mutton
Hammelkeule leg of mutton
Hammelrücken saddle of mutton
Handkäs mit Musik strong cheese in a salad dressing
Hartkäse hard cheese
Haschee hash
Hasenkeule haunch of hare
Hasenpfeffer hare casserole
Hauptspeisen main courses
Hecht pike
Heidelbeeren bilberries, blueberries
Heilbutt halibut
Heringsstipp herring salad
Heringstopf pickled herrings in sauce
Herz heart
Herzragout heart ragoût
Himbeeren raspberries

Himmel und Erde potato and apple purée with black pudding or liver sausage
Hirn brains
Hirschbraten roast venison
Honig honey
Honigmelone honeydew melon
Hoppelpoppel bacon and potato omelette
Hüfte haunch
Huhn chicken
Hühnerbrühe chicken broth
Hühnerfrikassee chicken fricassee
Hülsenfrüchte peas and beans, pulses
Hummer lobster
Ingwer ginger

J, K

Jägerschnitzel cutlet with mushrooms
Kabeljau cod
Kaffee coffee
Kaiserschmarren scrambled pancake with raisins
Kakao cocoa
Kalbfleisch veal
Kalbsbries sweetbread
Kalbsfrikassee veal ricassee
Kalbshaxe leg of veal
Kalbsnierenbraten roast veal with kidney
Kalbsschnitzel veal cutlet
kalte Platte cold platter
kaltes Büfett cold buffet
Kaltschale cold, sweet fruit soup
Kaninchen rabbit
Kapern capers
Karamelpudding caramel blancmange
Karotten carrots
Karpfen carp
Kartoffelbrei mashed potato
Kartoffeln potatoes

Kartoffelpuffer potato fritters

Kartoffelpüree mashed potato

Kartoffelsalat potato salad

Käse cheese

Käsegebäck cheese savouries

Käsekuchen cheesecake

Käseplatte selection of cheeses

Käse-Sahne-Torte cream cheesecake

Käsespätzle home-made noodles with cheese

Kasseler Rippenspeer smoked pork loin

Kasserolle casserole

Kassler smoked pork loin

Kastanien chestnuts

Katenrauchwurst smoked sausage

Keule leg, haunch

Kieler Sprotten smoked sprats

Kirschen cherries

klare Brühe consommé

Klöße dumplings

Knäckebrot crispbread

Knacker pork sausage for boiling or frying

Knackwurst pork sausage for boiling or frying

Knoblauch garlic

Knochen bone

Knochenschinken ham on the bone

Knödel dumplings

Kognak brandy

Kohl cabbage

Kohlrouladen stuffed cabbage leaves

Kohl und Pinkel cabbage, potatoes, sausage, and smoked meat

Kompott stewed fruit

Konfitüre jam

Königinpastete chicken vol-au-vent

Königsberger Klopse meatballs in caper sauce

Königskuchen type of fruit cake

Kopfsalat lettuce

Kotelett chop

Krabben shrimps; prawns

Krabbencocktail prawn cocktail

Kraftbrühe beef consommé

Kräuter herbs

Krautsalat coleslaw

Krautwickel stuffed cabbage leaves

Krebs crayfish

Kresse cress

Kroketten croquettes

Kruste crust

Kuchen cake

Kümmel caraway seeds

Kürbis pumpkin

L

Labskaus meat, fish, and potato stew

Lachs salmon

Lachsersatz cold smoked pollack (fish) dyed to look like salmon

Lachsforelle sea trout

Lachsschinken smoked rolled fillet of ham

Lamm lamb

Lammrücken saddle of lamb

Langusten crayfish

Lauch leek

Leber liver

Leberkäse baked pork and beef loaf

Leberpastete liver pâté

Leberwurst liver pâté

Lebkuchen gingerbread

Leinsamenbrot linseed bread

Leipziger Allerlei mixed vegetables

Linsen lentils

M

Mager lean
Mehrkornbrot multi-grain bread
Majoran marjoram
Makrele mackerel
Makronen macaroons
Mandeln almonds
mariniert marinaded, pickled
Markklößchen marrow dumplings
Marmelade jam
Maronen sweet chestnuts
Matjes(hering) young herring
Medaillons small fillets
Meeresfische seafish
Meeresfrüchte seafood
Meerrettich horseradish
Miesmuscheln mussels
Milch milk
Milchmixgetränk milk shake
Milchreis rice pudding
Mineralwasser mineral water
Mohnkuchen poppyseed cake
Möhren carrots
Mohrrüben carrots
Most fruit wine
Mus purée
Muscheln mussels
Muskat(nuss) nutmeg
MWSt (Mehrwertsteuer) VAT

N

nach Art des Hauses house special
nach Hausfrauenart home-made
Nachspeisen desserts
Nachtisch dessert
Napfkuchen ring-shaped poundcake
natürlich natural
Nieren kidneys
Nudeln pasta, noodles
Nüsse nuts

O

Obstsalat fruit salad
Ochsenschwanzsuppe oxtail soup
Öl oil
Oliven olives
Orangen oranges
Orangensaft orange juice

P

Palatschinken filled pancakes
paniert breaded
Paprika peppers, paprika
Paprikaschoten peppers
Paradiesäpfel tomatoes
Pastete vol-au-vent
Pellkartoffeln potatoes boiled in their jackets
Petersilie parsley
Pfannkuchen pancake(s)
Pfeffer pepper
Pfifferlinge chanterelles
Pfirsiche peaches
Pflaumen plums
Pflaumenkuchen plum tart
Pflaumenmus plum jam
Pichelsteiner Topf vegetable stew with beef
pikant spicy
Pilze mushrooms
Platte selection
pochiert poached
Pökelfleisch salt meat
Pommes frites French fried potatoes
Porree leek
Potthast braised beef with sauce
Poularde large chicken
Preiselbeeren cranberries
Presskopf brawn
Pumpernickel black rye bread
Püree purée, e.g. mashed potato
püriert puréed
Putenschenkel turkey leg
Puter turkey

Q, R

Quark curd cheese
Radieschen radishes
Rahm (sour) cream
Räucheraal smoked eel
Räucherhering kipper, smoked herring
Räucherlachs smoked salmon
Räucherspeck smoked bacon
Rauchfleisch smoked meat
Rehbraten roast venison
Rehgulasch venison goulash
Rehkeule haunch of venison
Rehrücken saddle of venison
Reibekuchen potato pancake
Reis rice
Reisbrei creamed rice
Reisrand with rice
Remoulade mayonnaise flavoured with herbs, mustard, and capers
Renke whitefish
Rettich radish
Rhabarber rhubarb
Rheinischer Sauerbraten roast pickled beef
Rinderbraten pot roast
Rinderfilet fillet steak
Rinderrouladen beef olives
Rinderzunge ox tongue
Rindfleisch beef
Rippchen spareribs
Risi-Pisi rice and peas
Roggenbrot rye bread
roh raw
Rohkostplatte selection of salads
Rollmops rolled-up pickled herring, rollmops
rosa rare to medium
Rosenkohl Brussels sprouts
Rosinen raisins
Rostbraten roast
Rostbratwurst barbecued sausage

Rösti fried potatoes and onions
Röstkartoffeln fried potatoes
Rotbarsch type of perch
Rote Bete beetroot
rote Grütze red berry compôte
Rotkohl red cabbage
Rotkraut red cabbage
Rotwein red wine
Rühreier scrambled eggs
Russische Eier egg mayonnaise

S

Sahne cream
Salate salads
Salatplatte selection of salads
Salatsoße salad dressing
Salz salt
Salzburger Nockerl(n) sweet soufflé
Salzheringe salted herrings
Salzkartoffeln boiled potatoes
Salzkruste salt crust
Sandkuchen type of Madeira cake
sauer sour
Sauerbraten roast pickled beef
Sauerkraut pickled white cabbage
Sauerrahm sour cream
Schaschlik (shish-)kebab
Schattenmorellen morello cherries
Schellfisch haddock
Schildkrötensuppe real turtle soup
Schillerlocken hot smoked dogfish
Schinken ham
Schinkenröllchen rolled ham
Schlachtplatte boiled pork and sausages with pickled cabbage and boiled potatoes

Schlagsahne whipped cream
Schlei tench
Schmorbraten pot roast
Schnecken snails
Schnittlauch chives
Schnitzel breaded escalope
Schokolade chocolate
Scholle plaice
Schulterstück shoulder piece
Schupfnudeln pasta made from potatoes and flour
Schwarzbrot dark rye bread
Schwarzwälder Kirschtorte Black Forest gâteau
Schwarzwurzeln salsify
Schwein pig
Schweinebauch belly of pork
Schweinefleisch pork
Schweinerippe cured pork chop
Schweinerollbraten rolled roast of pork
Schweineschmorbraten pot roast pork
Schweineschnitzel breaded pork cutlet
Schweinshaxe knuckle of pork
Seelachs pollack (fish)
Seezunge sole
Sekt sparkling wine
Sellerie celeriac, celery
Semmel bread roll
Senf mustard
Senfsahnesoße creamy mustard sauce
Senfsoße mustard sauce
Serbisches Reisfleisch paprika rice with cubed pork, peppers and onions
Soleier pickled eggs
Soße sauce, gravy
Soufflé soufflé
Spanferkel suckling pig
Spargel asparagus
Spätzle home-made pasta noodles

Speck fatty bacon
Speisekarte menu
Spezialität des Hauses house speciality
Spiegeleier fried eggs
Spießbraten joint roasted on a spit
Spinat spinach
Spitzkohl white cabbage
Springerle cookies
Sprotten sprats
Sprudel(wasser) mineral water
Stachelbeeren gooseberries
Stangen(weiß)brot French bread
Steinbutt turbot
Steinpilze cep mushrooms
Stollen Christmas fruit loaf
Strammer Max ham and fried egg on bread
Streuselkuchen cake with crumble topping
Sülze brawn
Suppen soups
Suppengrün mixed herbs and vegetables (used in soup)
süß sweet
süß-sauer sweet-and-sour
Süßspeisen sweet dishes
Süßwasserfische freshwater fish
Szegediner Gulasch goulash with pickled cabbage

T

Tafelwasser (still) mineral water
Tafelwein table wine
Tagesgericht dish of the day
Tageskarte menu of the day
Tagessuppe soup of the day
Tatar steak tartare
Taube pigeon
Tee tea
Teigmantel pastry case
Thunfisch tuna
Tintenfisch squid
Tomaten tomatoes

Törtchen tart(s)
Torte gâteau
Truthahn turkey

U, V

überbacken au gratin
Ungarisches Gulasch Hungarian goulash
ungebraten not fried
Vanille vanilla
Vanillesoße vanilla sauce
verlorene Eier poached eggs
Vollkornbrot dark whole grain bread
vom Grill grilled
vom Kalb veal
vom Rind beef
vom Rost grilled
vom Schwein pork
Vorspeisen hors d'oeuvres, starters

W

Waffeln waffles
Waldorfsalat salad with celery, apples, and walnuts
Wasser water
Wassermelone watermelon
Weichkäse soft cheese
Weinbergschnecken snails
Weinbrand brandy
Weincreme pudding with wine
Weinschaumcreme creamed pudding with wine
Weinsoße wine sauce
Weintrauben grapes
Weißbier wheat beer
Weißbrot white bread
Weißkohl white cabbage
Weißkraut white cabbage
Weißwein white wine
Weißwurst veal sausage
Weizenbier fizzy, light-coloured beer made with wheat
Wiener Schnitzel veal in breadcrumbs

Wild game
Wildschweinkeule haunch of wild boar
Wildschweinsteak wild boar steak
Windbeutel cream puff
Wirsing savoy cabbage
Wurst sausage
Würstchen frankfurter(s)
Wurstplatte selection of sausages
Wurstsalat sausage salad
Wurstsülze sausage brawn
würzig spicy

Z

Zander pike-perch, zander
Zigeunerschnitzel veal escalope with peppers, mushrooms, onions in tomato sauce
Zimt cinnamon
Zitrone lemon
Zitronencreme lemon cream
Zucchini courgettes
Zucker sugar
Zuckererbsen mangetout
Zunge tongue
Zungenragout tongue ragoût
Zutaten ingredients
Zwetche/Zwetschge type of plum
Zwiebelbrot onion bread
Zwiebeln onions
Zwiebelringe onion rings
Zwiebelsuppe onion soup
Zwiebeltorte onion tart
Zwischengerichte entrées

DICTIONARY ENGLISH–GERMAN

The gender of German nouns is shown by the word for "the": **der** (masculine), **die** (feminine), and **das** (neuter). **Die** is also used with plural nouns: **(m pl)**, **(f pl)** and **(n pl)** are used to show their gender. Some nouns change endings; here the masculine form is shown, with the feminine ending in brackets.

A

about **etwa**
accident **der Unfall**
accident and emergency department **die Unfallstation**
account number **die Kontonummer**
adapter **der Adapter**
address **die Adresse**
adult **die Erwachsene**
aerobics **das Aerobic**
aeroplane **das Flugzeug**
after **nach**
afternoon **der Nachmittag**
again **wieder**
air conditioning **die Klimaanlage**
air stewardess **die Flugbegleiterin**
airbag **der Airbag**
airmail **die Luftpost**
airport **der Flughafen**
aisle seat **der Gangplatz**
all **alle(s)**
allergic **allergisch**
almost **fast**
alone **allein**
already **bereits**
alright **in Ordnung**
ambulance **der Krankenwagen**
and **und**
ankle **der Knöchel**
another (different) **andere**
another (one more) **noch ein(e)**
answering machine **der Anrufbeantworter**
antibiotics **die Antibiotika**

anything **irgendetwas**
apartment **die Wohnung**
appointment **der Termin**
April **April**
apron **die Schürze**
arm **der Arm**
arm rest **die Armlehne**
armband; bracelet **das Armband**
arrivals hall **die Ankunftshalle**
arrive (verb) **ankommen**
art **die Kunst**
art gallery **das Kunstmuseum**
arthritis **die Arthrose**
artificial sweetener **der Süßstoff**
as (like) **wie**
asthma **das Asthma**
at **auf; an; in**
audio guide **der Audioführer**
August **August**
Australia **Australien**
automatic ticket machine **der Fahrscheinautomat**
autumn **der Herbst**
awful **furchtbar**

B

baby **das Baby**
babysitting **das Babysitten**
back (body) **der Rücken**
back (not front of) **die Rückseite**
backpack **der Rucksack**
bad **schlecht**
bag **die Tasche**
baggage **das Gepäck**
baggage allowance **das Freigepäck**

baggage reclaim die Gepäckausgabe
baker's der Bäcker
baking tray das Backblech
balcony; gallery der Balkon
ball der Ball
ballet das Ballett
bandage der Verband
bank die Bank
bank account das Bankkonto
bank holiday der Feiertag
bank manager der Bankdirektor
bar die Bar
barbecue der Grill
baseball das Baseball
baseball mitt der Baseballhandschuh
basket der Korb
basketball das Basketball
bath das Bad
bath robe der Bademantel
bathroom das Badezimmer
battery die Batterie
be (verb) sein
be lost (verb) sich verirren
beach der Strand
beach ball der Strandball
beach umbrella der Sonnenschirm
beautiful schön
bed das Bett
bee die Biene
beer das Bier
before vor
begin (verb) beginnen
beginner der Anfänger(in)
behind hinter
below unter
belt der Gürtel
beneath unterhalb
beside neben
bicycle das Fahrrad
bidet das Bidet
big groß
bikini der Bikini
bill die Rechnung
black schwarz
blanket die Decke

bleeding die Blutung
blender der Mixer
blood pressure der Blutdruck
blood test die Blutprobe
blue blau
boarding gate der Flugsteig
boarding pass die Bordkarte
boat trip die Schifffahrt
boat das Schiff
body der Körper
body lotion die Körperlotion
bonnet (car) die Mütze
book das Buch
book (verb) buchen
book shop der Buchladen
boot (car) der Kofferraum
boot (footwear) der Stiefel
bottle die Flasche
bottle opener der Flaschenöffner
boutique die Boutique
bowl der Schüssel
box die Schachtel
boy der Junge
boyfriend der Freund
breakdown die Panne
breakfast das Frühstück
bridge die Brücke
briefcase die Aktentasche
British britisch
broken gebrochen
brooch die Brosche
bruise die Prellung
brush der Handbesen
bubblebath das Schaumbad
bucket der Eimer
bumper die Stoßstange
burgle (verb) einbrechen
burn die Verbrennung
bus der Bus
bus station der Busbahnhof
bus stop die Bushaltestelle
business das Geschäft
bust die Büste
but aber
butcher's der Metzger
butter die Butter
buy (verb) kaufen
by bis

C

cable car die Seilbahn
café das Café
calm ruhig
camera die Kamera
camera bag die Kameratasche
camp (verb) kampieren
camping kettle der Wasserkocher
camping stove der Gaskocher
campsite der Campingplatz
can (noun) die Dose
can (verb) können
can opener der Dosenöffner
Canada Kanada
canoe das Kanu
capsule die Kapsel
car das Auto
car crash der Verkehrsunfall
car park der Parkplatz
car rental die Autovermietung
car stereo das Autoradio
caravan der Wohnwagen
caravan site der Wohnwagenplatz
carry (verb) tragen
cash das Bargeld
cash machine der Geldautomat
casino das Kasino
castle das Schloss
cathedral der Dom
CD die CD
central heating die Zentralheizung
centre das Zentrum
chair lift der Sessellift
change das Kleingeld
change (money) wechseln
changing room die Umkleidekabine
channel (TV) der Fernsehkanal
charge (verb) berechnen; verlangen
cheap billig
check in (verb) einchecken

check-out (supermarket) die Kasse
cheek die Wange
cheers! prost!
cheque der Scheck
cheque card die Scheckkarte
chequebook das Scheckbuch
chest die Brust
chewing gum der Kaugummi
child das Kind
child seat der Kindersitz
chin das Kinn
chopping board das Hackbrett
church die Kirche
cigarette die Zigarette
cinema das Kino
city die (Groß)stadt
clean sauber
clean (verb) säubern
cleaner die Putzfrau
close (near) nah
close (verb) schließen
closed geschlossen
clothes die Kleidung
cloudy bewölkt
coast die Küste
coat der Mantel
coat hanger der Kleiderbügel
colander das Sieb
cold (adj) kalt
cold (illness) der Schnupfen
colour die Farbe
colouring pencil der Farbstift
come (verb) kommen
comic der Comic
compartment das Abteil
compass der Kompass
complain (verb) sich beschweren
computer der Computer
concert das Konzert
concourse die Bahnhofshalle
conditioner die Pflegespülung

constipation die Verstopfung
consul der Konsul
consulate das Konsulat
contact number die Rufnummer
contents der Inhalt
coolbox die Kühlbox
corkscrew der Korkenzieher
cot das Kinderbett
couchette der Liegeplatz
cough der Husten
country das Land
courier der Kurier
course der Kurs
credit card die Kreditkarte
crime das Verbrechen
crockery die Töpferware
cross trainer der Ellipsentrainer
cufflinks die Manschettenknöpfe (m pl)
cup die Tasse
cut der Schnitt
cutlery das Besteck
cycle helmet der Fahrradhelm

D

damaged beschädigt
dancing das Tanzen
daughter die Tochter
day der Tag
December Dezember
deck chair der Liegestuhl
deep tief
degrees die Grade (m pl)
delayed verspätet
delicatessen der Delikatessenladen
delicious köstlich
dentist der Zahnarzt
deodorant das Deodorant
departure board die Abflugtafel
departures hall die Abflughalle
deposit die Anzahlung
dessert das Dessert
detergent das Waschpulver

develop (film) entwickeln
diabetic Diabetiker(in) (m/f)
diarrhoea der Durchfall
diesel der diesel
digital camera die Digitalkamera
dinner das Abendessen
disabled parking der Behindertenparkplatz
disabled person Behinderte(r) (f/m)
dish die Schüssel
divorced geschieden
doctor der Arzt
doctor's surgery die Arztpraxis
dog der Hund
doll die Puppe
door die Tür
double bed das Doppelbett
double room das Doppelzimmer
drawing die Zeichnung
dress das Kleid
drink (noun) das Getränk
drink (verb) trinken
drive (verb) fahren
driving licence der Führerschein
dry trocken
during während
dust pan das Kehrblech
dustbin die Mülltonne
duty-free shop der Duty Free Shop
DVD player der DVD-Spieler

E

each jeder
ear das Ohr
early früh
east der Osten
easy leicht
eat (verb) essen
egg das Ei
eight acht
elbow der Ellbogen
electric razor der Rasierapparat

electrician der Elektriker

electricity der Strom

email die E-Mail

email address die E-Mail-Adresse

embassy die Botschaft

emergency services die Notdienste (m pl)

empty leer

engine der Motor

English (language) Englisch

English Engländer(in) (m/f)

engraving der Stich

enjoy (verb) genießen

entrance der Eingang

entrance ticket die Eintrittskarte

envelope der Briefumschlag

epileptic Epileptiker(in) (m/f)

equipment die Ausrüstung

euro der Euro

evening der Abend

every jeder

examine (verb) untersuchen

exchange rate der Wechselkurs

excursion der Ausflug

exercise bike der Heimtrainer

exhaust (car) der Auspuff

exit der Ausgang

expensive teuer

express service der Express-Service

extension lead das Verlängerungskabel

extra extra

eye das Auge

F

face das Gesicht

fairground der Rummelplatz

family die Familie

family room das Familienzimmer

family ticket die Familienkarte

fan der Ventilator

far weit

fare der Fahrpreis

fast schnell

father der Vater

February Februar

feel (verb) fühlen

ferry die Fähre

fill (verb) füllen

film der Film

find (verb) finden

fine (legal) die Strafe

finger der Finger

finish (verb) beenden

fire alarm der Feueralarm

fire brigade die Feuerwehr

fire engine das Feuerwehrauto

fire extinguisher der Feuerlöscher

firefighter der Feuerwehrmann

first erste

fishing das Angeln

fishmonger der Fischhändler

five fünf

fix (verb) befestigen; festlegen

flash gun das Blitzgerät

flash photography das Fotografieren mit Blitzlicht

flight der Flug

flight meal die Flugmahlzeit

flip-flop die Flip-Flops (f pl)

flippers die Flossen (f pl)

float das Schwimmkissen

flu die Grippe

fly (verb) fliegen

food das Essen

foot der Fuß

football der Fußball

for für

forget (verb) vergessen

fork die Gabel

form die Form

four vier

fracture der Bruch

free frei

fresh frisch

Friday Freitag

fridge-freezer der Gefrier-Kühlschrank

friend Freund(in) (m/f)
from von; aus
frying pan die Bratpfanne
fuel gauge die Benzinuhr
full voll
furniture shop das Möbelgeschäft
fuse box der Sicherungskasten

G

game das Spiel
garage die Werkstatt
garden der Garten
gas das Gas
gate das Tor
gear stick die Kupplung
get (verb) bekommen
gift das Geschenk
gift shop die Geschenkboutique
gift-wrap (verb) als Geschenk verpacken
girl das Mädchen
girlfriend die Freundin
give (verb) geben
glass das Glas
glasses die Brille
gloss der Glanz
go (verb) gehen
go for a walk (verb) spazieren gehen
go out (verb) ausgehen
go shopping (verb) einkaufen gehen
goggles die Schutzbrille
golf das Golfspiel
golf ball der Golfball
golf club der Golfclub
golf course der Golfplatz
golf tee das Golf-Tee
good evening Guten Abend!
good night Gute Nacht!
good gut
goodbye Auf Wiedersehen!
grater die Reibe
Great Britain Großbritannien
green grün
greengrocer der Gemüsehändler

grill pan die Grillpfanne
group die Gruppe
guarantee die Garantie
guest der Gast
guide der Führer
guidebook der Reiseführer
guided tour die Besichtigungstour
gym das Fitnessstudio

H

hair das Haar
hairdryer der Föhn
half die Hälfte
hand die Hand
hand luggage das Handgepäck
handbag die Handtasche
handle der Griff
happen (verb) geschehen
happy froh
harbour der Hafen
hardware shop das Haushaltswarengeschäft
hatchback der Hecktürmodell
hate (verb) hassen
have (verb) haben
hay fever der Heuschnupfen
hazard lights die Warnleuchten (f pl)
he er
head der Kopf
head rest die Kopfstütze
headache die Kopfschmerzen
headlight der Scheinwerfer
health die Gesundheit
health insurance die Krankenversicherung
hear (verb) hören
heart condition die Herzkrankheit
heater der Heizlüfter
heating die Heizung
heel (foot) die Ferse
hello Hallo!
help (verb) helfen
her ihr(e)

here **hier**
high blood pressure **der hohe Blutdruck**
high chair **der Kinderstuhl**
high-speed train **der Hochgeschwindig-keitszug**
hiking **das Wandern**
hire (verb) **leihen; mieten**
hold (verb) **halten**
holdall **die Reisetasche**
holiday **der Urlaub**
home **das Heim**
horn (car) **die Hupe**
horse riding **das Reiten**
hospital **das Krankenhaus**
hot **heiß**
hotel **das Hotel**
hour **die Stunde**
house **das Haus**
hovercraft **das Hovercraft**
how? **wie?**
how many? **wie viel(e)?**
humid **feucht**
hurry (verb) **beeilen**
husband **der Ehemann**
hydrant **der Hydrant**
hydrofoil **das Tragflügelboot**

I

I **ich**
ice **das Eis**
icy **eisig**
ID **der Ausweis**
ill **krank**
illness **die Krankheit**
in front of **vor**
inhaler **der Inhalator**
injection **die Spritze**
injure (verb) **verletzen**
insect repellent **das Insektenschutzmittel**
insurance **die Versicherung**
insurance company **die Versicherungsgesellschaft**
insurance policy **die Versicherungspolice**
intensive care unit **die Intensivstation**
interesting **interessant**

internet **das Internet**
internet café **das Internetcafé**
interpreter **Dolmetscher(in) (m/f)**
inventory **das Inventar**
iPod **der iPod**
iron **das Bügeleisen**
ironing board **das Bügelbrett**
it **er; sie; s**
Italian **italienisch(m)/(f)**
Italy **Italien**

J

jacket **die Jacke**
January **Januar**
jaw **der Kiefer**
jazz club **der Jazzclub**
jeans **die Jeans (f pl)**
jellyfish **die Qualle**
jeweller's **der Juwelier**
jewellery **der Schmuck**
July **Juli**
jumper **der Pullover**
June **Juni**

K

keep (verb) **behalten**
kettle **der Wasserkessel**
key **der Schlüssel**
keyboard **die Tastatur**
kidney **die Niere**
kilo **das Kilo**
kilometre **der Kilometer**
kitchen **die Küche**
knee **das Knie**
knife **das Messer**
knock down **niederschlagen**
know (facts) **wissen**
know (people) **kennen**

L

lake **der See**
laptop **der Laptop**
last **letzte**
late **spät**
lawyer **Rechtsanwalt(in) (m/f)**
leak **das Leck**
leave (verb) **verlassen**

left (direction) links
left luggage die Gepäcksaufbewahrung
leg das Bein
lens die Linse
life jacket die Schwimmweste
lifebuoy der Rettungsring
lifeguard der Rettungsschwimmer
lift der Lift
lift pass der Liftpass
light (adj) hell
light (noun) das Licht
light (verb) beleuchten
light bulb die Glühbirne
lighter das Feuerzeug
lighthouse der Leuchtturm
list die Liste
listen (verb) zuhören
little klein
local lokal; örtlich
lock das Schloss
log on (verb) einloggen
log out (verb) ausloggen
long lang
look (verb) schauen
lose (verb) verlieren
lost property das Fundamt
love (verb) lieben
luggage das Gepäck
lunch das Mittagessen

M

magazine die Zeitschrift
mail die Post
mallet der Holzhammer
make (verb) machen
man der Mann
manual das Handbuch
manuscript das Manuskript
marina der Jachthafen
market der Markt
married verheiratet
match (light) das Streichholz
match (sport) das Match; das Spiel
matt matt
mattress die Matratze
May Mai

meal die Mahlzeit
mechanic Mechaniker(in) (m/f)
medicine die Medizin
medium mittelgroß
memory card die Memory Card
memory stick der Memory Stick
mend ausbessern
message die Nachricht
microwave die Mikrowelle
midday der Mittag
middle die Mitte
midnight die Mitternacht
mini bar die Minibar
minute die Minute
mistake der Fehler
misty nebelig
mixed gemischt
mobile phone das Handy
mole das Muttermal
Monday Montag
money das Geld
month der Monat
monument das Denkmal
mop der Mopp
more mehr
morning der Morgen
mother die Mutter
motorbike das Motorrad
motorway die Autobahn
mountain der Berg
mountain bike das Mountainbike
mouse (computer) die Maus
mouth der Mund
mouthwash das Mundwasser
much viel
museum das Museum
music die Musik
musician Musiker(in) (m/f)
must (verb) müssen
my mein(e)

N

nail der Nagel
nail clippers die Nagelzange
nail scissors die Nagelschere

name der Name
napkin die Serviette
nausea die Übelkeit
near nah
neck der Nacken
necklace die Halskette
need (verb) brauchen
never nie
new neu
newspaper die Zeitung
next nächste
next to neben (da)
nice hübsch; angenehm
night die Nacht
nightclub der Nachtclub
nine neun
no nein
north der Norden
nose die Nase
nosebleed das Nasenbluten
not nicht
nothing nichts
November November
number die Zahl
number plate das
   Nummernschild
nurse die
   Krankenschwester

O

October Oktober
of von
off aus
often oft
oil das Öl
ointment die Salbe
on auf
on board an Bord
one eins
online Online
only nur
open offen
open (verb) öffnen
opening hours die
   Öffnungszeiten (f pl)
opera die Oper
opera house das Opernhaus
operation die Operation
opposite gegenüber
or oder

orange (colour) orange
order die Bestellung
our unser
out aus
outside außerhalb
oven der Backofen
over über
owe (verb) schulden

P

pain der Schmerz
painkiller das Schmerzmittel
painting das Gemälde
pair das Paar
paper das Papier
papers (identity) die Papiere
   (n pl)
parcel das Paket
park der Park
parking meter die Parkuhr
passenger der Passagier
passport der Pass
passport control die
   Passkontrolle
pay (verb) zahlen
pay in (verb) einzahlen
pedestrian crossing der
   Fußgängerübergang
peeler der Schäler
pen der Füller
pencil der Bleistift
people die Menschen (m pl)
perhaps vielleicht
personal CD player der
   CD-Spieler
pet das Haustier
petrol das Benzin
petrol station die Tankstelle
pharmacist Apotheker(in)
   (m/f)
pharmacy die Apotheke
phone das Telefon
phone card die Telefonkarte
photo album das Fotoalbum
photo frame der
   Fotorahmen
photograph das Foto
photography die Fotografie
pianist Pianist(in) (m/f)
picnic das Picknick

picnic hamper das Picknickkorb
piece das Stück
pilates das Pilates
pill die Pille; die Tablette
pillow das Kopfkissen
pilot Pilot(in) (m/f)
pink rosa
PIN-number die Geheimzahl
plaster das Pflaster
plate der Teller
platform der Bahnsteig
play das Theaterstück
play (games) spielen
playground der Spielplatz
please bitte
plug der Stecker
police die Polizei
police car das Polizeiauto
police station die Polizeiwache
policeman der Polizist
policewoman die Polizistin
porter der Gepäckträger
possible möglich
post office das Postamt
postbox der Briefkasten
postcard die Postkarte
postman der Briefträger
prefer (verb) vorziehen
pregnant schwanger
prescription das Rezept
price der Preis
print (photo) der Abzug
print (verb) drucken
pump die Pumpe
puncture die Reifenpanne
purse der Geldbeutel
put (verb) stellen

Q

quarter das Viertel
quick schnell
quite ganz
quite ziemlich

R

radiator der Heizkörper
radio das Radio
railway die Eisenbahn

railway station der Bahnhof
rain (verb) regnen
rape die Vergewaltigung
rash der Ausschlag
razor das Rasiermesser
read (verb) lesen
ready fertig
really wirklich
reboot (verb) neu starten
receipt die Quittung
reclaim tag das Gepäcketikett
recommend (verb) empfehlen
record shop das Plattengeschäft
red rot
reduction die Ermäßigung
registration number die Zulassungsnummer
remote control die Fernbedienung
rent (verb) mieten
repair (verb) reparieren
replace (verb) ersetzen
report (verb) berichten
reserve (verb) reservieren
reservation die Reservierung
restaurant das Restaurant
restaurant car der Speisewagen
resuscitation die Wiederbelebung
retired pensioniert
return ticket die Rückfahrkarte
right (correct) richtig
right (direction) rechts
river der Fluss
road signs die Verkehrsschilder (n pl)
road die Straße
robbery der Raub
roll (film) die Rolle
roofrack der Dachgepäckträger
room das Zimmer
round rund
roundabout der Kreisverkehr

rowing machine die Rudermaschine

rubbish der Müll

rubbish bin der Mülleimer

S

safari park der Safaripark

safe sicher

sailing das Segeln

sailing boat das Segelboot

saloon car die Limousine

same gleich

sand der Sand

sandal die Sandale

satellite TV das Satellitenfernsehen

Saturday Samstag

saucepan der Kochtopf

saucer die Untertasse

say (verb) sagen

scan der Sanner

scissors die Schere

scooter der Roller

sea das Meer

season die Jahreszeit

seat der Sitz

seat belt der Sicherheitsgurt

second zweiter

second (time) die Sekunde

see (verb) sehen

sell (verb) verkaufen

sell-by date das Verfalldatum

send (verb) senden

senior citizen Senior(in) (m/f)

separately getrennt

September September

serious ernst

serve (verb) servieren

seven sieben

shampoo das Shampoo

shaving foam der Rasierschaum

she sie

shirt das Hemd

shoe der Schuh

shop das Geschäft

shopping mall das Einkaufszentrum

shorts die Shorts (m pl)

shoulder die Schulter

shower die Dusche

shower gel das Duschgel

side effect die Nebenwirkung

sign (verb) unterschreiben

signpost der Wegweiser

singer Sänger(in) (m/f)

single room das Einzelzimmer

single ticket die Einzelfahrt

six sechs

size die Größe

ski (verb) skifahren

ski boots die Skistiefel (m pl)

skiing der Skisport

skin die Haut

ski poles die Skistöcke (m pl)

skirt der Rock

skis die Skier (m pl)

sliproad die Zubringerstraße

slow langsam

small klein

smoke (verb) rauchen

smoke alarm der Rauchmelder

snack der Snack

snake die Schlange

sneeze (verb) nießen

snorkel der Schnorchel

snow (verb) schneien

snowboard das Snowboard

so so

soap die Seife

socks die Socken (f pl)

soft toy das Kuscheltier

some einige

somebody jemand

something etwas

sometimes manchmal

soon bald

sorry! entschuldigung!

south der Süden

souvenir das Souvenir

spare tyre der Ersatzreifen

speak (verb) sprechen

speciality die Spezialität

speed limit die
Geschwindigkeitsbegrenzung
speedometer der
Tachometer
splint die Schiene
splinter der Splitter
spoon der Löffel
sport der Sport
sports centre das
Sportzentrum
spray das Spray
sprain die Verstauchung
spring der Frühling
square (in town) der Platz
stairs die Treppe
stamp die Briefmarke
start (verb) starten
statue die Statue
stay (verb) bleiben
steering wheel das Lenkrad
step machine der Stepper
sterling das Pfund-Sterling
sticky tape der Klebestreifen
stolen gestohlen
stomach der Magen
stomach ache die
Magenschmerzen
stop! halt!
stop (verb) anhalten
stopcock der Absperrhahn
stormy stürmisch
straight on geradeaus
street map der Stadtplan;
die Straßenkarte
string die Schnur
strong stark
student Student(in) (m/f)
student card der
Studentenausweis
suit der Anzug
suitcase der Koffer
summer der Sommer
sun die Sonne
sun lounger die
Sonnenliege
sunburn der Sonnenbrand
Sunday Sonntag
sunglasses die Sonnenbrille
sunhat der Sonnenhut

sunny sonnig
sunscreen die
Sonnencreme
suntan lotion das
Sonnenschutzmittel
supermarket der
Supermarkt
suppositories das Zäpfchen
surf (verb) surfen
surfboard das Surfboard
sweet süß
swimming das Schwimmen
swimming goggles die
Schwimmbrille
swimming pool das
Schwimmbad
swimsuit der Badeanzug

T

table der Tisch
tablet die Tablette
tailor der Schneider
take (verb) nehmen
takeaway der Schnellimbiss
taxi das Taxi
taxi rank der Taxistand
teaspoon der Teelöffel
teeth die Zähne (m pl)
telephone das Telefon
telephone box die
Telefonzelle
television das Fernsehen
temperature die Temperatur
tennis das Tennis
tennis ball der Tennisball
tennis court der Tennisplatz
tennis racquet der
Tennisschläger
tent das Zelt
terminal das Terminal
thank (verb) danken
that/this dieser(e) (m/f)
the der(m) die(f); das(n)
theatre das Theater
their ihr(e)
theme park der Erlebnispark
then dann
there is/are es gibt
thermostat der Thermostat

thief der Dieb
thirty dreißig
think (verb) denken
three drei
throat Kehle(f)
through durch
thumb der Daumen
Thursday Donnerstag
ticket der Fahrschein
tight eng
time die Zeit
timetable der Fahrplan
to nach; zu; zum
tobacco der Tabak
tobacconist der
   Tabakwarenhändler
today heute
toe die Zehe
toilet die Toilette
toll die Maut
tomorrow morgen
tonight heute abend
too; also auch
toothache die
   Zahnschmerzen (m pl)
toothbrush die Zahnbürste
toothpaste die Zahnpaste
torch die Taschenlampe
tour die Rundreise
tour guide Reiseleiter(in)
   (m/f)
tourist Tourist(in) (m/f)
tourist information office das
   Fremdenverkehrsbüro
tow (verb) abschleppen
towel das Handtuch
town die Stadt
town centre das
   Stadtzentrum
town hall das Rathaus
toy das Spielzeug
traffic jam der Stau
traffic lights die
   Verkehrsampel
train der Zug
trainers die Turnschuhe
   (m pl)
traveller's cheque der
   Reisescheck
trolley der Kofferkuli

trousers die Hose
t-shirt das T-Shirt
Tuesday Dienstag
turn (verb) umdrehen
twenty zwanzig
twin beds zwei Einzelbetten
   (n pl)
two zwei
twelve zwölf
tyre der Reifen
tyre pressure der
   Reifendruck

U

umbrella der Schirm
underground railway die
   U-Bahn
underground station die
   U-Bahnstation
understand (verb) verstehen
United States die
   Vereinigten Staaten (m pl)
unleaded bleifrei
until bis
up oben
urgent dringend
us uns
use (verb) gebrauchen
useful nützlich
usual; usually gewöhnlich

V

vacate (verb) frei machen
vacuum cleaner der
   Staubsauger
vacuum flask die
   Thermosflasche
validate (verb) bestätigen
valuables die
   Wertgegenstände (m pl)
value Wert (m)
vegetarian Vegetarier(in)
   (m/f)
vehicle das Fahrzeug
venetian blind die Jalousie
very sehr
video game das Videospiel
view der Blick
village das Dorf
vineyard der Weinberg

visa **das Visum**
visit **der Besuch**
visitor **Besucher(in) (m/f)**

W

wait **warten**
waiter **der Ober**
waiting room **das Wartezimmer**
waitress **die Kellnerin**
wake-up call **der Weckruf**
walking boots **die Wanderschuhe (m pl)**
wallet **die Brieftasche**
want **möchten; wollen**
ward **die Krankenstation**
warm **warm**
washing machine **die Waschmaschine**
wasp **die Wespe**
watch (verb) **zusehen**
water **Wasser (n)**
waterfall **der Wasserfall**
waterproofs **die Regenbekleidung**
water-skiing **das Wasserskifahren**
way **der Weg**
we **wir**
weather **das Wetter**
website **die Website**
Wednesday **Mittwoch**
week **die Woche**
weekend **die Wochenende**
welcome **willkommen**
well (health) **gesund**
west **der Westen**
wet **nass**
what? **was?**
wheel **das Rad**
wheelchair access **der Zugang für Rollstuhlfahrer**
wheelchair ramp **die Rollstuhlrampe**
when? **wann?**
where? **wo?**
which? **welcher?**
whisk **der Schneebesen**
white **weiß**

who? **wer?**
why? **warum?**
wife **die Ehefrau**
wind **der Wind**
window seat **der Fensterplatz**
windscreen **die Windschutzscheibe**
windscreen wipers **die Scheibenwischer (m pl)**
windsurfing **das Windsurfing**
windy **windig**
wine **der Wein**
winter **der Winter**
with **mit**
withdrawal **die Abhebung**
without **ohne**
witness (noun) **Zeuge/Zeugin (m/f)**
woman **die Frau**
work **die Arbeit**
wrapping paper **das Geschenkpapier**
wrist **das Handgelenk**
wrist watch **die Armbanduhr**
wrong **falsch**

X, Y, Z

X-ray **die Röntgenaufnahme**
yacht **die Jach**
year **das Jahr**
yellow **gelb**
yes **ja**
yesterday **gestern**
yoga **das Joga**
you **du (singular informal); Sie (singular formal; plural)**
your **dein (singular informal); Ihr (singular formal; ihr (plural)**
zoo **der Zoo**

DICTIONARY GERMAN–ENGLISH

The gender of German nouns is shown by (m), (f), and (n) for masculine, feminine, and neuter singular nouns and (m pl), (f pl) and (n pl) for plural nouns. Some nouns, such as jobs, change endings according to gender. The masculine form is shown, followed by the feminine ending in brackets.

A

Abend (m) evening
Abendessen (n) dinner
Abflug (m) take off
Abflughalle (f) departures hall
abheben to withdraw
Abhebung (f) withdrawal
Absatz (m) heel (shoe)
abschleppen to tow
Absperrhahn (m) stopcock
Abteil (n) compartment
Abzug (m) print (photo)
acht eight
Adapter (m) adapter
Adresse (f) address
Aerobic (n) aerobics
Airbag (m) airbag
Aktentasche (f) briefcase
alle(s) all
allein alone
allergisch allergic
Amerikaner(in) (m/f) American
an at; by
andere another (different)
Anfänger(in) (m/f) beginner
Angeln (n) fishing
angenehm nice (pleasant)
anhalten to stop
ankommen to arrive
Ankunftshalle (f) arrivals hall
Anrufbeantworter (m) answering machine
Antibiotika (f) antibiotics
Anzahlung (f) deposit
Anzug (m) suit
Apotheke (f) pharmacy
Apotheker(in) (m/f) pharmacist

April (m) April
Arbeit (f) work
arbeiten to work
Arm (m) arm
Armband (n) armband; bracelet
Armlehne (f) arm rest
Arthrose (f) arthritis
Arzt (m) doctor
Arztpraxis (f) doctor's surgery
Asthma (n) asthma
auch too; also
Audioführer (m) audio guide
auf on; at
Auf Wiedersehen! goodbye
aufgeben to post
Auge (n) eye
August (m) August
aus from; off; out
Ausflug (m) excursion
Ausflugsboot (n) pleasure boat
Ausgang (m) exit
ausgehen to go out
ausloggen to log out
Auspuff (m) exhaust (car)
Ausrüstung (f) equipment
Ausschlag (m) rash
außerhalb outside
austauschen exchange
Australien Australia
Australier(in) (m/f) Australian
Ausweis (m) ID
Auto (n) car
Autobahn (f) motorway
Autoradio (n) car stereo
Autovermietung (f) car rental

B

Babysitten (n) babysitting
Backblech (n) baking tray
Bäcker (m) baker's
Backofen (m) oven
Bad (n) bath
Badeanzug (m) swimsuit
Bademantel (m) bath robe
Badezimmer (n) bathroom
Bahnhof (m) railway station
Bahnhofshalle (f) concourse
Bahnsteig (m) platform
bald soon
Balkon (m) balcony; gallery
Ball (m) ball
Ballett (n) ballet
Bank (f) bank
Bankdirektor (m) bank manager
Bankkonto (n) bank account
Bar (f) bar
Bargeld (n) cash
Baseballhandschuh (m) baseball mitt
Basketball (n) basketball (game)
Batterie (f) battery
beeilen to hurry
beenden to finish
befestigen to fix
beginnen to begin
behalten to keep
Behinderte(r) (f/m) disabled person
Behindertenparkplatz (m) disabled parking
Beilage (f) side dish
Bein (n) leg
bekommen to get
beleuchten to light
Benzin (n) petrol
Benzinuhr (f) fuel gauge
berechnen to charge
bereits already
Berg (m) mountain
Bericht (m) report
berichten to report
beschädigt damaged

beschweren: sich beschweren to complain
Besichtigungstour (f) guided tour
bestätigen to validate
Besteck (n) cutlery
Bestellung (f) order
Besuch (m) visit
Besucher(in) (m/f) visitor
Bett (n) bed
bewölkt cloudy
Bidet (n) bidet
Biene (f) bee
Bier (n) beer
Bikini (m) bikini
billig cheap
bis until
bis by; until
bitte please
blau blue
bleiben to stay
bleifrei unleaded
Bleistift (m) pencil
Blick (m) view
Blitzgerät (n) flash gun
Blutdruck(m) blood pressure
Blutprobe (f) blood test
Blutung (f) bleeding
Bordkarte (f) boarding pass
Botschaft (f) embassy
Boutique (f) boutique
Bratpfanne(f) frying pan
brauchen to need
Breitbildfernseher (m) widescreen TV
Briefkasten (m) postbox
Briefmarke (f) stamp
Brieftasche (f) wallet
Briefträger (m) postman
Briefumschlag (m) envelope
Brille (f) glasses
britisch British
Bruch (m) fracture
Brust (f) chest
Buch (n) book
buchen to book
Buchladen (m) book shop
Bügelbrett (n) ironing board

Bügeleisen (n) iron
Bürste (f) brush
Bus (m) bus
Busbahnhof (m) bus station
Bushaltestelle (f) bus stop
Büste (f) bust
Butter (f) butter

C, D

Café (n) café
Campingplatz (m) campsite
CD (f) CD
CD-Spieler (m) CD player
Check-in (m) check-in
Comic (m) comic
Computer (m) computer
Dachgepäckträger (m) roofrack
danken to thank
dann then
das (n) the
Daumen (m) thumb
Decke (f) blanket
dein your
Delikatessenladen (m) delicatessen
denken to think
Denkmal (n) monument
Deodorant (n) deodorant
der (m) the
Dessert (n) dessert
Dessertlöffel (m) dessertspoon
Dezember (m) December
Diabetiker(in) (m/f) diabetic
die (f) the
Dieb (m) thief
Dienstag (m) Tuesday
diesel (m) diesel
dieser/e/es (m/f/n) this
Digitalkamera (f) digital camera
Dolmetscher(in) (m/f) interpreter
Dom (m) cathedral
Donnerstag (m) Thursday
Doppelbett (n) double bed
Doppelzimmer (n) double room

Dorf (n) village
Dose (f) can (noun)
Dosenöffner (m) can opener
drei three
dringend urgent
drucken to print
du you
durch through
Durchfall (m) diarrhoea
Dusche (f) shower
Duschgel (n) shower gel
Duty Free Shop (m) duty-free shop
DVD-Player (m) DVD player

E

Ehefrau (f) wife
Ehemann (m) husband
Ei (n) egg
Eimer (m) bucket
einbrechen to burgle
einchecken to check in
Eingang (m) entrance
einige some
einkaufen gehen to go shopping
Einkaufszentrum (n) shopping mall
einloggen to log on
eins one (number)
Eintrittskarte (f) entrance ticket
einzahlen to pay in
Einzelfahrt (f) single ticket
Einzelzimmer (n) single room
Eis (n) ice
Eisenbahn (f) railway
eisig icy
Elektriker (m) electrician
Ellbogen (m) elbow
Ellipsentrainer (m) cross trainer
E-Mail (f) email
E-Mail-Adresse (f) email address
empfehlen to recommend
eng tight

Engländer(in) (m/f) English
Englisch English (language)
entschuldigung! sorry!
entwickeln to develop (film)
Epileptiker(in) (m/f) epileptic
er he; it
Erlebnispark (m) theme park
Ermäßigung (f) reduction
ernst serious
Ersatzreifen (m) spare tyre
ersetzen to replace
erste first
Erwachsene (m/f) adult
es it
es gibt there is/are
essen to eat
Essen (n) food
etwa about; approximately
etwas something
Euro (n) euro
Express-Service (m) express service
extra extra

F

Fähre (f) ferry
fahren to drive
Fahrgeschäfte (n pl) rides
Fahrplan (m) timetable (train)
Fahrpreis (m) fare
Fahrrad (n) bicycle
Fahrradhelm (m) cycle helmet
Fahrradpumpe (f) bicycle pump
Fahrradschloss (n) cycle lock
Fahrschein (m) ticket (train)
Fahrscheinautomat(m) automatic ticket machine
Fahrzeug (n) vehicle
falsch wrong
Familie (f) family
Familienkarte (f) family ticket
Familienzimmer (n) family room

Farbe (f) colour
Farbstift (m) colouring pencil
fast almost
Februar (m) February
Fehler (m) mistake
Feiertag (m) bank holiday
Fensterplatz (m) window seat
Fernbedienung (f) remote control
Fernsehen (n) television
Fernsehkanal (m) channel (TV)
Ferse (f) heel
fertig ready
festlegen to fix
feucht humid
Feueralarm (m) fire alarm
Feuerlöscher (m) fire extinguisher
Feuerwehr (f) fire brigade
Feuerwehrauto (n) fire engine
Feuerwehrmann (m) firefighter
Feuerzeug (n) lighter
Film (m) film
finden to find
Finger (m) finger
Fisch (m) fish
Fischhändler (m) fishmonger
Fitness-Studio (n) gym
Flasche (f) bottle
Flaschenöffner (m) bottle opener
fliegen to fly
Flip-Flops (f pl) flip-flop
Flossen (f pl) flippers
Flug (m) flight
Flugbegleiterin (f) air stewardess
Flughafen (m) airport
Flugmahlzeit (f) flight meal
Flugsteig (m) boarding gate
Flugzeug (n) aeroplane
Fluss (m) river
Föhn (m) hairdryer
Form (f) form

Foto (n) photograph
Fotoalbum (n) photo album
Fotografie (f) photography
Fotografieren mit Blitzlicht (n) flash photography
Fotorahmen (m) photo frame
Frau (f) woman
frei free
Freibad (n) outdoor pool
Freigepäck (n) baggage allowance
Freitag (m) Friday
Fremdenverkehrsbüro (n) tourist information office
Freund(in) (m/f) friend
frisch fresh
froh happy
Frucht (f) fruit
früh early
Frühling (m) spring
Frühstück (n) breakfast
Führer (m) guide
Führerschein (m) driving licence
füllen to fill
Fundamt (n) lost property
fünf five
für for
furchtbar awful
Fuß (m) foot
Fußball (m) football
Fußgängerübergang (m) pedestrian crossing

G

Gabel (f) fork
Gangplatz (m) aisle seat
ganz quite
Garantie (f) guarantee
Garten (m) garden
Gas (n) gas
Gaskocher (m) camping stove
Gast (m) guest
geben to give
gebrauchen to use
gebrochen broken
Gefrier-Kühlschrank (m) fridge-freezer

gegenüber opposite
Geheimzahl (f) PIN-number
gehen to go
gelb yellow
Geld (n) money
Geldautomat (m) cash machine
Geldbeutel (m) purse
Gemälde (n) painting
gemischt mixed
Gemüsehändler (m) greengrocer
genießen to enjoy
Gepäck (n) luggage
Gepäckausgabe(f) baggage reclaim
Gepäcketikett (n) reclaim tag
Gepäcksaufbewahrung (f) left luggage
Gepäckträger (m) porter
geradeaus straight on
Geschäft (n) business
Geschäft (n) shop
geschehen to happen
Geschenk (n) gift
Geschenkboutique (f) gift shop
Geschenkpapier (n) wrapping paper
geschieden divorced
geschlossen closed
Geschwindigkeits-begrenzung (f) speed limit
Gesicht (n) face
Gespräch (m) phone call
gestern yesterday
gestohlen stolen
gesund well (health)
Gesundheit (f) health
Getränk (n) drink (noun)
getrennt separately
gewöhnlich usual; usually
Glanz (m) gloss
Glas (n) glass
gleich same
Glühbirne (f) light bulb
Golfball (m) golf ball
Golfclub (m) golf club

Golfplatz (m) golf course
Golfspiel (n) golf
Golf-Tee (n) golf tee
Grade (m pl) degrees
Griff (m) handle
Grill (m) barbecue
Grillpfanne (f) grill pan
Grippe (f) flu
groß big; large
Großbritannien Great Britain
Größe (f) size
(Groß)stadt (f) city
grün green
Gruppe (f) group
Gürtel (m) belt
gut good; well
Gute Nacht! Good night
Guten Abend! Good evening

H

Haar (n) hair
haben to have
Hackbrett (n) chopping board
Hafen (m) harbour
Hälfte (f) half
Hallenbad (n) indoor pool
Hallo! hello
Halskette (f) necklace
halten to hold
Haltestelle (f) bus stop
Hand (f) hand
Handbesen (m) brush
Handbuch (n) manual
Handgelenk (n) wrist
Handgepäck (n) hand luggage
Handtasche (f) handbag
Handtuch (n) towel
Handy (n) mobile phone
hassen to hate
Haus (n) house
Haushaltswarengeschäft (n) hardware shop
Haustier (n) pet
Haut (f) skin
Handbuch (n) manual
Hecktürmodell (n) hatchback

Heim (n) home
Heimtrainer (m) exercise bike
heiß hot
Heizkörper (m) heater; radiator
Heizung (f) heating
helfen to help
hell light (adj)
Hemd (n) shirt
Herbst (m) autumn
Hering (m) tent peg
Herzkrankheit (f) heart condition
Heuschnupfen (m) hay fever
heute today
heute abend tonight
hier here
hinter behind
Hochgeschwindigkeitszug (m) high-speed train
hohe Blutdruck (m) high blood pressure
Holzhammer (m) mallet
hören to hear
Hotel (n) hotel
Hovercraft (n) hovercraft
hübsch nice (attractive)
Hund (m) dog
Hupe (f) horn (car)
Husten (m) cough
Hydrant (m) hydrant

I

ich I
ihm, ihn him
Ihr your
ihr(e) her; their
in at; in
Inhalator (m) inhaler
Inhalt (m) contents
Insektenschutzmittel (n) insect repellent
Intensivstation (f) intensive care unit
interessant interesting
Interesse(n) interest
Internet (n) internet

Internetcafé (n) internet café
Inventar (n) inventory
iPod (m) iPod
irgendeiner someone
irgendetwas anything
Italien Italy
italienisch Italian

J

ja yes
Jacht (f) yacht
Jachthafen (m) marina
Jacke (f) jacket
Jahr (n) year
Jahreszeit (f) season
Jalousie (f) venetian blind
Januar (m) January
Jazzclub (m) jazz club
Jeans (f pl) jeans
jeder each
jemand somebody
Jetski (m) jet ski
Joga (n) yoga
Juli (m) July
Junge (m) boy
Juni (m) June
Juwelier (m) jeweller

K

kalt cold (adj)
Kamera (f) camera
Kameratasche (f) camera bag
kampieren to camp
Kanada Canada
Kanu (n) canoe
Kapsel (f) capsule
Kasino (n) casino
Kasse (f) check-out
kaufen to buy
Kaugummi (m) chewing gum
Kehle (f) throat
Kehrblech (n) dustpan
Kellnerin (f) waitress
kennen to know (people)
Kiefer (m) jaw
Kilo (n) kilo
Kilometer (m) kilometre

Kind (n) child
Kinderbett (n) cot
Kindersitz (m) child seat
Kinderstuhl (m) high chair
Kinn (n) chin
Kino (n) cinema
Kirche (f) church
Klebestreifen (m) sticky tape
Kleid (n) dress
Kleiderbügel (m) coat hanger
Kleidung (f) clothes
klein little
klein small
Kleingeld (n) change
Klimaanlage (f) air con
Knie (n) knee
Knöchel (m) ankle
Kochtopf (m) saucepan
Koffer (m) suitcase
Kofferkuli (m) trolley
Kofferraum (m) boot (car)
kommen to come
Kompass (m) compass
können to be able to
Konsul (m) consul
Konsulat (n) consulate
Kontonummer (f) account number
Konzert (n) concert
Kopf (m) head
Kopfkissen (n) pillow
Kopfschmerzen (f) headache
Kopfstütze (f) head rest
Korb (m) basket
Korkenzieher (m) corkscrew
Körper (m) body
Körperlotion (f) body lotion
köstlich delicious
krank ill
Krankenhaus (n) hospital
Krankenschwester (f) nurse
Krankenstation (f) hospital ward
Krankenversicherung (f) health insurance
Krankenwagen (m) ambulance

Krankheit (f) illness
Kreditkarte (f) credit card
Kreisverkehr (m) roundabout
Küche (f) kitchen
Kühlbox (f) coolbox
Kunst (f) art
Kunstmuseum (n) art gallery
Kupplung (f) gear stick
Kurier (m) courier
Kurs (m) course
Kuscheltier (n) soft toy
Küste (f) coast

L

Land (n) country
lang long
langsam slow
Laptop (m) laptop
Leck (n) leak
leer empty
legen to put
leihen to hire
Lenkrad (n) steering wheel
lesen to read
letzte last
Leuchtturm (m) lighthouse
Licht (n) light
lieben to love
Liegeplatz (m) couchette; mooring
Liegestuhl (m) deck chair
Lift (m) lift
Liftpass (m) lift pass
Limousine (f) saloon car
links left
Linse (f) lens
Löffel (m) spoon
lokal local
Luftpost (f) airmail

M

machen to make
Mädchen (n) girl
Magen (m) stomach
Magenschmerzen (f) stomach ache
Mahlzeit (f) meal
Mai (m) May

manchmal sometimes
Mann (m) man
Manschettenknöpfe (m pl) cufflinks
Mantel (m) coat
Manuskript (n) manuscript
Markt (m) market
Maschine (f) machine
Match (n) match (sport)
Matratze (f) mattress
matt matt
Maus (f) mouse (computer)
Maut (f) toll
Mechaniker(in) (m/f) mechanic
Medizin (f) medicine
Meer (n) sea
mehr more
mein(e) my
Memory Card (f) memory card
Memory Stick (m) memory stick
Menschen (m pl) people
Messer (n) knife
Metzger (m) butcher's
mieten to hire
mieten to rent
Mikrowelle (f) microwave
Minibar (f) mini bar
Minute (f) minute
mit with
Mittag (m) midday
Mittagessen (n) lunch
Mitte (f) middle
mittelgroß medium
Mitternacht (f) midnight
Mittwoch (m) Wednesday
Mixer (m) blender
Möbelgeschäft (n) furniture shop
mögen to want
möglich possible
Monat (m) month
Montag (m) Monday
Mopp (m) mop
morgen tomorrow
Morgen (m) morning
Motor (m) engine
Motorrad (n) motorbike

Mountainbike (n) mountain bike
Müll (m) rubbish
Mülleimer (m) rubbish bin
Mund (m) mouth
Mundwasser (n) mouthwash
Museum (n) museum
Musik (f) music
Musiker(in) (m/f) musician
müssen to have to
Mutter (f) mother
Muttermal (n) mole (medical)
Mütze (f) bonnet

N

nach after
nach to
Nachmittag (m) afternoon
Nachricht (f) message
nächste next
Nacht (f) night
Nachtclub (m) nightclub
Nacken (m) neck
Nagel (m) nail
Nagelschere (f) nail scissors
Nagelzange (f) nail clippers
nah close (near)
nah near
Name (m) name
Nase (f) nose
Nasenbluten (n) nosebleed
nass wet
nebelig misty
neben beside
neben (da) next to
Nebenwirkung (f) side effect
nehmen to take
nein no
neu new
neun nine
neu starten to reboot
nicht not
nichts nothing
nie never
niederschlagen knock down
Niere (f) kidney
nießen to sneeze

noch ein(e) another
Norden (m) north
Notdienste (m pl) emergency services
November (m) November
Nummernschild (n) number plate
nur only
nützlich useful

O

oben up
Ober(m) waiter
oder or
offen open
öffnen to open
Öffnungszeiten (f pl) opening/ visiting hours
oft often
ohne without
Ohr (n) ear
Oktober (m) October
Öl (n) oil
Online online
Oper (f) opera
Operation (f) operation
Opernhaus (n) opera house
orange orange (colour)
Ordnung: in Ordnung alright; fine; OK
örtlich local
Osten (m) east

P

Paar (n) pair
Paket (n) packet; parcel
Panne (f) breakdown
Papier (n) paper
Papiere (n pl) papers (identity)
Park (m) park
Parkplatz (m) car park
Parkuhr (f) parking meter
Pass (m) passport
Passagier (m) passenger
Passkontrolle (f) passport control
pensioniert retired
Pflaster (n) plaster

Pflegespülung (f) conditioner

Pfund-Sterling (n) sterling

Pianist(in) (m/f) pianist

Picknick (n) picnic

Picknickkorb (m) picnic hamper

Pilates (n) pilates

Pille (f) pill

Pilot(in) (m/f) pilot

Plattengeschäft (n) record shop

Platz (m) square (in town)

Police (f) policy

Polizei (f) police

Polizeiwache (f) police station

Polizist (m) policeman

Polizistin (f) policewoman

Postamt (n) post office

Postkarte (f) postcard

Preis (m) price

Prellung (f) bruise

Programm (n) programme

prost! cheers!

Pullover (m) jumper

Pumpe (f) pump

Puppe (f) doll

Putzfrau (f) cleaner

Q, R

Qualle (f) jellyfish

Quittung (f) receipt

Rad (n) wheel

Radio (n) radio

Rasierapparat (m) electric razor

Rasiermesser (n) razor

Rasierschaum (m) shaving foam

Rathaus (n) town hall

Raub (m) robbery

rauben to rob

rauchen to smoke

Rauchmelder (m) smoke alarm

Rechnung (f) bill

rechts right (direction)

Rechtsanwalt(in) (m/f) lawyer

Regenbekleidung (f) waterproofs

regnen to rain

Reibe (f) grater

Reifen (m) tyre

Reifendruck (m) tyre pressure

Reifenpanne (f) puncture

Reiseführer (m) guidebook

Reiseleiter(in) (m/f) tour guide

reisen to travel

Reisescheck (m) traveller's cheque

Reisetasche (f) holdall

Reiten (n) horse riding

reparieren to repair

reservieren to reserve

Reservierung (f) reservation

Restaurant (n) restaurant

Rettungsring (m) lifebuoy

Rettungsschwimmer(m) lifeguard

Rezept (n) prescription

Rezeption (f) reception (hotel)

richtig right; correct

Rock (m) skirt

Rolle (f) roll of film

Roller (m) scooter

Rollstuhlrampe (f) wheelchair ramp

Röntgenaufnahme (f) X-ray

rosa pink

rot red

Rücken (m) back (body)

Rückfahrkarte (f) return ticket

Rucksack (m) backpack

Rückseite (f) back (not front of)

Rudermaschine (f) rowing machine

Rufnummer (f) contact number

ruhig calm

Rummelplatz (m) fairground

rund round

Rundreise (f) tour

S

Safaripark (m) safari park
sagen to say; to tell
Salbe (f) ointment
Samstag (m) Saturday
Sand (m) sand
Sandale (f) sandal
Sänger(in) (m/f) singer
Sanner (m) scan
Satellitenfernsehen (n) satelliteTV
sauber clean
säubern to clean
Schachtel (f) box
Schäler (m) peeler
Schalter (m) desk
schauen to look
Schaumbad (n) bubblebath
Scheck (m) cheque
Scheckbuch (n) chequebook
Scheckkarte (f) cheque card
Scheibenwischer (m pl) windscreen wipers
Scheinwerfer (m) headlight
Schere (f) scissors
Schiene (f) splint
Schiff (n) boat; ship
Schifffahrt(f) boat trip
Schirm (m) umbrella
Schlange (f) snake
schlecht bad
schließen to close
Schloss (n) castle; lock
Schlüssel (m) key
Schmerz (m) pain
Schmerzmittel (n) painkiller
Schmuck (m) jewellery
Schneebesen (m) whisk
Schneider (m) tailor
schneien to snow
schnell fast; quick
Schnellimbiss (m) takeaway
Schnitt (m) cut
Schnorchel (m) snorkel
Schnupfen (m) cold
Schnur (f) string
schön beautiful
Schuh (m) shoe
schulden to owe

Schulter (f) shoulder
Schürze (f) apron
Schüssel (f) dish
Schüssel (n) bowl
Schutzbrille (f) goggles
schwanger pregnant
schwarz black
Schwimmbad (n) swimming pool
Schwimmbrille (f) swimming goggles
Schwimmen (n) swimming
Schwimmkissen (n) float
Schwimmweste (f) life jacket
See (m) lake
sechs six
Segelboot (n) sailing boat
Segeln (n) sailing
sehen to see
sehr very
Seife (f) soap
Seilbahn (f) cable car
Sekunde (f) second
selbst myself
senden to send
Senior(in) (m/f) senior citizen
September (m) September
servieren to serve
Serviette (f) napkin
Sessellift (m) chair lift
setzen to put
Shampoo (n) shampoo
Shorts (m pl) shorts
sicher safe
Sicherungskasten (m) fuse box
sie she; they
Sie you
Sieb (n) colander
sieben seven
Sitz (m) seat
sitzen to sit
Skier (m pl) skis
skifahren to ski
Skisport (m) skiing
Skistiefel (m pl) ski boots
Skistöcke (m pl) ski poles
Snack (m) snack

Snowboard (n) snowboard

so so

Socken (f pl) socks

Sommer (m) summer

Sonne (f) sun

Sonnenbrand (m) sunburn

Sonnenbrille (f) sunglasses

Sonnencreme (f) sunscreen

Sonnenhut (m) sunhat

Sonnenliege (f) sun lounger

Sonnenschirm (m) beach umbrella

Sonnenschutzmittel (n) suntan lotion

sonnig sunny

Sonntag (m) Sunday

Souvenir (n) souvenir

Spachtel (m) spatula

spät late

Speisewagen (m) restaurant car

Spezialität (f) speciality

Spiel (n) match (sport)

Spiel (n) game

spielen to play (games)

Spielplatz (m) playground

Spielzeug (n) toy

Splitter (m) splinter

Sport (m) sport

Sportzentrum (n) sports centre

Spray (n) spray

sprechen to speak; to talk

Spritze (f) injection

Stadt (f) town

Stadtplan (m) streetmap

Stadtzentrum (n) town centre

stark strong

starten to start

Statue (f) statue

Stau (m) traffic jam

Stecker (m) plug

stellen to put

Stepper (m) step machine

Stich (m) engraving

Stiefel (m) boot

Stoßstange (f) bumper

Strafe (f) fine (legal)

Strand (m) beach

Strandball (m) beach ball

Straße (f) road; street

Straßenkarte (f) street map

Streichholz (n) match (light)

Streifenwagen (m) police car

Strom (m) electricity

Stück (n) piece; slice

Student(in) (m/f) student

Studentenausweis (m) student card

Stunde (f) hour

stürmisch stormy

Süden (m) south

Supermarkt (m) supermarket

surfen to surf

süß sweet

Süßstoff (m) artificial sweetener

T

Tabak (m) tobacco

Tabakwarenhändler (m) tobacconist

Tablette (f) tablet; pill

Tachometer (m) speedometer

Tag (m) day

Tankstelle (f) petrol station

Tanzen (n) dancing

Tasche (f) bag

Taschenlampe (f) torch

Tasse (f) cup

Tastatur (f) keyboard

Taxi (n) taxi

Taxistand (m) taxi rank

Teelöffel (m) teaspoon

Telefonkarte (f) phone card

Telefonzelle (f) telephone box

Teller (m) plate

Temperatur (f) temperature

Tennis (n) tennis

Tennisball (m) tennis ball

Tennisplatz (m) tennis court

Tennisschläger (m) tennis racquet

Termin (m) appointment

Terminal (n) terminal

teuer expensive
Theater (n) theatre
Theaterstück (n) play
Thermosflasche (f)
  vacuum flask
Thermostat (m) thermostat
Tisch (m) table
Tochter (f) daughter
Toilette (f) toilet
Toilettenpapier (n) toilet
  paper
Töpferware (f) crockery
Tor (n) gate
Tourist(in) (m/f) tourist
tragen to carry
Tragflügelboot (n) hydrofoil
Treppe (f) stairs
trinken to drink
trocken dry
T-Shirt (n) t-shirt
Tür (f) door
Turnschuhe (m pl) trainers

U

U-Bahn (f) underground
  railway
U-Bahnstation (f)
  underground station
Übelkeit (f) nausea
über over; across; more than
überholen to overtake
Uhr (f) clock; watch; o'clock
umdrehen to turn
Umkleidekabine (f)
  changing room
und and
Unfall (m) accident
Unfallstation (f) Accident
  and Emergency
  department
unmöglich impossible
uns us
unser our
unter below
unterhalb beneath
unterschreiben to sign
untersuchen to examine
Untertasse (f) saucer
Urlaub (m) holiday

V

Vater (m) father
Vegetarier(in) (m/f)
  vegetarian
Ventilator (m) fan
Verband (m) bandage;
  dressing
Verbrechen (n) crime
Verbrennung (f) burn
Vereinigten Staaten (m pl)
  United States
Verfalldatum (n)
  sell-by date
vergessen to forget
Vergewaltigung (f) rape
verheiratet married
verkaufen to sell
Verkehrsampel (f) traffic
  lights
Verkehrsschilder (n pl)
  road signs
Verkehrsunfall (m)
  car crash
verlangen to charge
Verlängerungskabel (n)
  extension lead
verlassen to leave
verletzen to injure
verlieren to lose
Versicherung (f) insurance
Versicherungsgesellschaft
  (f) insurance company
Versicherungspolice (f)
  insurance policy
verspätet delayed
Verstauchung (f) sprain
verstehen to understand
Verstopfung (f)
  constipation
versuchen to try
Videospiel (n) video game
viel a lot; much
vielleicht perhaps
vier four
Viertel (n) quarter
Visum (n) visa
voll full
von from; of
vor before; in front of
vorziehen to prefer

W

während during
Wandern (n) hiking
Wanderschuhe (m pl) walking boots
Wange (f) cheek
wann? when?
warm warm
Warnleuchten (f pl) hazard lights
warten to wait
Wartezimmer (n) waiting room
warum? why?
was? what?
Waschmaschine (f) washing machine
Waschpulver (n) detergent
Wasser (n) water
Wasserfall (m) waterfall
Wasserkessel (m) kettle
Wasserskifahren (n) water-skiing
Website (f) website
Wechselkurs (m) exchange rate
wechseln to change
Weckruf (m) wake-up call
Weg (m) way
Wegweiser (m) signpost
Weinberg (m) vineyard
weiß white
weit far
welcher? which?
wer? who?
Werkstatt (f) garage
Wertgegenstände (m pl) valuables
Wespe (f) wasp
Westen (m) west
Wetter (n) weather
wie as; how?
wie viel(e)? how many?
wieder again
Wiederbelebung (f) resuscitation
willkommen welcome
windig windy
Windschutzscheibe (f) windscreen

Windsurfer (m) windsurfer
Winter (m) winter
wir we; us
wirklich really
wissen to know (facts)
wo? where?
Woche (f) week
Wochenende (n) weekend
Wohnung (f) apartment
Wohnwagen (m) caravan
Wohnwagenplatz (m) caravan site
wollen to want

Z

Zahl (f) number
zahlen to pay
Zahnarzt (m) dentist
Zahnbürste (f) toothbrush
Zähne (m pl) teeth
Zahnpaste (f) toothpaste
Zahnschmerzen (m pl) toothache
Zäpfchen (n) suppository
Zehe (f) toe
Zeichnung (f) drawing
Zeit (f) time
Zeitschrift (f) magazine
Zeitung (f) newspaper
Zelt (n) tent
Zentralheizung (f) central heating
Zentrum (n) centre
ziemlich quite
Zigarette (f) cigarette
Zimmer (n) room
Zoo (m) zoo
zu to
Zubringerstraße (f) sliproad
Zug (m) train
Zugang für Rollstuhlfahrer (m) wheelchair access
zuhören to listen
zum; zur to
zusehen to watch
zwanzig twenty
zwei two
zwei Einzelbetten (n pl) twin beds
zweiter second

ACKNOWLEDGMENTS

Dorling Kindersley would like to thank the
following for their help in the preparation of this
book: Elma Aquino and Mandy Earey for design
assistance; Nicola Hodgson for editorial assistance;
Claire Bowers, Lucy Claxton, and Rose Horridge
in the DK Picture Library; Adam Brackenbury,
Vânia Cunha, Almudena Diaz, Maria Elia,
John Goldsmid, Sonia Pati, Phil Sergeant, and
Louise Waller for DTP assistance.

PICTURE CREDITS

Key: a (above); b (below/bottom); c (centre);
l (left); r (right); t (top)

Alamy Images: PhotoSpin, Inc p36 crb; vario
images GmbH & Co.KG p94 b; Hayden Richard
Verry p111 cb; WoodyStock p59 clb;
Courtesy of Renault: p24–25 t;
Getty Images: Reggie Casagrande p146;
PunchStock: Moodboard p6

Jacket images: *Front:* Getty Images: GK Hart/Vikki
Hart c. *Back:* Getty Images: Panoramic Images

All other images © **Dorling Kindersley**
For further information, see: **www.dkimages.com**